A LEVEL
Questions and Answers

BUSINESS STUDIES

Martin Clinton

Senior Examiner

SERIES EDITOR: BOB McDUELL

Letts

EDUCATIONAL

Contents

Introduction

HOW TO USE THIS BOOK

The aim of the *Questions and Answers* series is to provide the student with the help required to attain the highest level in one of the most important examinations – the Advanced Level General Certificate of Education (GCE) or, in Scotland, the Higher Grade Scottish Certificate of Education (SCE). The books are designed to help all students up to A grade. The series relies on the premise that an experienced Examiner can provide, through examination questions, sample answers and advice, the help a student needs to secure success. Many revision aids concentrate on providing factual information which might have to be recalled in an examination. This series, while giving factual information in an easy-to-remember form, concentrates on the other skills which need to be developed for GCE and SCE examinations.

The *Questions and Answers* series is designed to provide:

- Easy-to-use **Revision Summaries** which identify important factual information. These are to remind you, in summary form, of the topics you will need to have revised in order to answer examination questions.

- Advice on the different types of question in each subject and how to answer them well to obtain the highest marks.

- Information about other skills, apart from the recall of knowledge, which will be tested in examination papers. These are sometimes called **Assessment Objectives**. Modern GCE and SCE examinations put great emphasis on the testing of other objectives apart from knowledge and understanding. Typically, questions testing these Assessment Objectives can make up over 50% of the mark allocated to written papers. Assessment Objectives include analysis, decision making, communication, problem solving, data handling, evaluation and interpretation (see p.5 for more details). The *Questions and Answers* series is intended to develop these skills by the use of questions and by showing how marks are allocated.

- Many examples of **examination questions**. Students can improve their results by studying a sufficiently wide range of questions, providing they are shown the way to improve their answers to these questions. It is advisable that students try these questions first before going to the answers and the advice which accompanies the answers. All of the questions come from actual examination papers.

- **Sample answers** to all of the questions.

- **Advice from Examiners**. By using the experience of actual Examiners, we are able to give advice which can enable students to see how their answers can be improved and success ensured.

Success in GCE and SCE examinations comes from proper preparation and a positive attitude to the examination, developed through a sound knowledge of facts and an understanding of principles. The books are intended to overcome 'examination nerves', which often come from a fear of not being properly prepared.

THE IMPORTANCE OF USING QUESTIONS FOR REVISION

Past examination questions play an important part in revising for examinations. However, it is important not to start practising questions too early. Nothing can be more disheartening than trying to do a question which you do not understand because you have not mastered the topic. Therefore, it is important to have studied a topic thoroughly before attempting any questions on it.

How can past examination questions provide a way of preparing for the examination? It is unlikely that any question will appear in exactly the same form on the papers you are going to take. However, the examiner is restricted on what he can set as questions must cover the whole syllabus and test certain Assessment Objectives. The number of totally original questions you can set on any part of the syllabus is very limited and so similar ideas occur over and over again. It certainly will help you if the question you are trying to answer in an examination is familiar and you know you have done similar questions before. This is a great boost for your confidence and confidence is what is required for examination success.

Practising examination questions will also highlight gaps in your knowledge and understanding which you can go back and revise more thoroughly. It will also indicate which sorts of questions you can do well and which, if there is a choice of questions, you should avoid.

Attempting past questions will get you used to the type of language used in questions.

Finally, having access to answers, as you do in this book, will enable you to see clearly what is required by the examiner, how best to answer each question, and the amount of detail required. Attention to detail is a key aspect of achieving success at A Level.

MAXIMISING YOUR MARKS

One of the keys to examination success is to know how marks are gained and lost by candidates. There are two important aspects to this: ensuring you follow the instructions (or 'rubric') on the examination paper and understanding how papers are marked by examiners.

Often candidates fail to gain the marks they deserve because they do not follow the rubric exactly. If you are asked to answer four questions from a section and you answer five, you can only receive credit for four. The examiner may be instructed to mark the first four only and cross out additional questions. It would be unfortunate if the fifth was your best. Anyway, attempting too many questions means you will have wasted time. You cannot have spent the correct amount of time on each of the four questions and your answers could have suffered as a result.

Where a choice of questions is possible, candidates often choose the wrong questions. A question which looks familiar may not always be as easy as it seems and valuable time can be lost going up 'dead-ends'. If you have a choice, spend time reading all of the questions and making rough notes before you start. Then start with the questions you think you can do the best and leave any you are not sure about until later when, hopefully, your confidence will have grown. When choosing, look at the marks allocated to various parts of the questions and try to judge if you are confident in those parts where most marks are available.

For every examination paper there is a mark scheme, which tells the examiner where marks should and should not be awarded. For example, where a *knowledge-based* question is worth a maximum of five marks, there will be five, six or maybe more correct marking points and the examiner will award the first five given by the candidate. A '(5)' shown after a question on an exam paper is an indication that five points are required from your answer. Obviously, lengthy writing will not gain credit unless the candidate is hitting the right responses. Try therefore to keep your answers brief and to the point. Look at your answers critically after you have written them and try to decide how many different important points you have made. Advice on marking schemes for questions that test more than just recall of knowledge is given on p.5 under 'Levels-based marking schemes'.

An important principle of examination marking is called consequential marking (also called 'own figure' marking). This means that if a candidate makes a mistake, the examiner must only penalise the candidate for it once. For example, if you made a mistake early in a calculation so that you came up with an incorrect value, you would obviously lose a mark. However, if you then used this incorrect value in a later part of the question, and your working was correct apart from this incorrect value, you would not lose any more marks. Therefore, always write down all of your workings, so that you can gain marks even if you make an early slip up. You will see examples of consequential marking in the questions in this book.

TYPES OF EXAMINATION QUESTION

In Advanced Level Business Studies, your knowledge and skills are likely to be examined by four types of question. These are short-answer, data response, case study and essays. Details of each of these are given below. Several examination boards will ask relatively easy factual recall questions at the start of an examination paper. Their purpose is to ease you into the examination by calming your nerves with questions which rely mainly on memory skills. These questions are referred to as short-answer questions. They often require one word or one sentence answers. You should not spend too long on this section or write too much. If you do not know an answer move on and return to it at the end of the examination. However, because this is A Level a larger part of the examination will be testing your abilities to apply the skills and knowledge you have learnt in your Business Studies Course.

Data response questions

Data response questions are a common form of testing application. They usually comprise two or three fairly structured questions based on a particular piece of data (information). The data will normally be fairly short and may be verbal, numerical or both. Most examination boards try to keep this information up to date and real. So the data might be a short extract from a newspaper article or a firm's accounts. One important tip here is that if you regularly read good newspapers (the main paper is probably more important than the business section) you will be more familiar with the language used on data papers and are more likely to write good answers. Data questions are likely to be on a specific topic but you may mix topics and such is the integrated nature of Business Studies that you should use all the skills you have learnt. The key to answering data questions is to read the questions carefully so that you answer the questions set. The answer is almost certainly contained in the data so that it must be read and analysed thoroughly. Do take notice of how many marks are awarded to each of the questions and allocate your time accordingly.

Case studies

A more extensive test of application and analysis is set using the case study. Boards vary in their use of the case studies. Some use lengthy articles from Business Magazines, others create detailed fictional businesses with masses of information, yet others produce fairly short (one side of A4) fictional businesses. Another significant difference is that some boards pre-release a case study some weeks before the examination and others expect the candidate to tackle the case study when seeing it for the first time in the examination room. In the latter situation, skim-read the case study in order to be able to put it into context. You should then read the questions making sure you understand what they mean and what the Examiner is looking for. You should then return to read the case study very carefully, highlighting key words and phrases which provide the evidence for answering the questions. Having found the evidence, you should ask yourself if it is convincing (does it answer the question)! You should then write a brief plan of your answer to give it structure. The case study tests your decision-making skills. You will often read about firms facing particular problems and you may have to decide how to tackle the problem. You will have to weigh up evidence and hence your evaluation skills are being tested. The case study will almost certainly involve some testing of numerical skills, e.g. working out cost, revenues and profits, drawing break-even charts, cash-flow forecasts, even depreciation calculations. You should not be afraid of these. The calculations are often simple if you have taken the time to learn these relatively simple concepts thoroughly. If the case study has been pre-released you will be expected to have analysed it thoroughly. You should have been through it word by word ensuring you are familiar with any business terminology or concepts used.

Essay questions

The final and fairly familiar form of assessment is the essay question. Essays test the whole range of skills but are particularly good at testing synthesis and evaluation. Synthesis shows that you have really taken Business Studies on board and see it in a holistic fashion. Successful business activity is an integrated activity. All the different parts of businesses interact and affect each other. Even if an essay appears to be an essay about a marketing decision there are bound to be implications for personnel, production, accounts etc. Evaluation is regarded as the highest order skill, but you possessed this skill even when you were very young. Evaluation means making judgements, weighing up arguments, distinguishing between fact and opinion, looking at the pros and cons of a particular decision.

The author has developed with the help of his students a mnemonic for remembering what is required in an essay. He calls this the **seven C's** of essay writing. In terms of style, three of the C's are being **concise**, **coherent** and **convincing**. That is, you should not waffle. Many students believe that essays are marked on length, but it is quality not quantity that counts. Examiners can spot when you are padding out an essay. Once you have gained a mark for a particular point it cannot be awarded again however often it is repeated in however many different ways. Incidentally, short sentences are best and certainly you should never put more than one point in a sentence. If you draw up an essay plan this will give the essay structure and enable it to be coherent. It is often-repeated advice, but an essay should have an introduction, a middle and a conclusion. You should refer to the question and be certain you are answering it. If you are not certain the answer is right how are you going to convince the Examiner?

Your decision at the start of the examination over which essays to answer should have been made on the basis of which you could answer most convincingly, and writing out essay plans should avoid the catastrophe of getting half way through an essay before realising that you do not know the answer. Timing is very important. You should have read the rubric (the rules of the examination) thoroughly so you know how many questions you have to answer and how long to spend on each. You should make a note of when you started answering an essay and what time you should finish. You must be disciplined and stop at that time. You are likely to gain many more marks for the time spent on the next essay than any additional marks you might have gained on the essay on which you over-ran. This is an example of opportunity cost, a concept with which you should be familiar!

The other four C's are **cases**, **content**, **critical understanding** and **conclusion**. Cases refers to the fact that you should use lots of examples in your essays. Business Studies is a living, up to date subject and you should be able to apply your knowledge of theory to the real world. Examiners will expect to see references to current economic and business events. Marks are awarded for relevant examples. Content refers to the knowledge of business concepts, terminology and techniques that you will have to use in answering the essay. Critical understanding is about the application and analysis of these ideas in a particular question. This may involve questioning the relevance of a piece of theory or a particular point of view if the essay title is a quote from one side of a current business debate. There is nearly always more than one right answer and always more than one perspective on a problem. Conclusion refers to the evaluation skills discussed above.

ASSESSMENT OBJECTIVES

These are the skills you will be tested on through the examination questions. You will be expected to:

- Demonstrate a **knowledge** of the main terminology and principles related to syllabus content, i.e. the ability to recall specific terms, techniques, principles and facts;
- Demonstrate a **critical understanding** of the complex and changing situations in business. Comprehension skills will be demonstrated by the appropriate **selection**, **interpretation** and **manipulation** of business information and data (in written, graphical and numerical forms);
- **Organise** and **apply** information to business problems. This will involve application of business knowledge to explain unfamiliar business matters and situations;
- Be able to **analyse** business problems, being able to break down information into what is important and unimportant and being able to distinguish between fact and opinion. You should have skills of **synthesis**, being able to reorganise information, to test a hypothesis and to make generalisations;
- Be able to use skills of **evaluation**, i.e. make reasoned judgments, reach suitable conclusions and communicate them appropriately.

LEVELS-BASED MARKING SCHEMES

You will see in the answers section of this book that examination boards have begun to use levels-based marking schemes. The idea behind this is to reward the use of the skills outlined above. Your ability to explain, analyse and evaluate is more important than just repeating memorized facts. The levels are linked with an increasing number of marks, hence there are often more levels in questions with more marks. The lowest levels are associated with the easiest skills, e.g. just listing a series of points. To move into the next level you may have to *explain* the points. For the level after this the ability to *analyse* may be required. The highest level (often only available on essay questions) is awarded for *evaluation*. Within each level you gain more marks depending on the quality of your answer.

1 *Business organisations*

REVISION SUMMARY

You should be familiar with all the different types of trading organisations in both the **private sector** and the **public sector**. Private sector organisations are owned by individuals and often aim to make a profit for individuals. However, charities and mutual societies are in the private sector, and they aim to give away any surpluses they make from trading. Mutual societies such as Building Societies are owned by their customers for their benefit. Public sector organisations are owned by the whole population and run on our behalf by the Government. But non-trading public services such as Social Services are quite different from public corporations like British Rail. British rail could be run as a private sector industry aiming to make a profit.

You should also know of any recent trends in ownership, especially if they are unusual or controversial. A business practice which is a current trend is a very likely examination question. For example, in the 1990s several examination boards had questions on **franchising**, **privatisation**, **mergers**, **management buy-outs** and reverting to **private limited company** status.

You should know how the aims of organisations differ, and how they take different approaches to similar problems. You should have knowledge of the main features of each business type and the constraints which are particular to that type of organisation.

In the private sector you should know **one-person businesses**, **partnerships**, **private limited companies**, **public limited companies**, **cooperatives**, **franchises**, **multinationals** and **charities**. In the public sector you should know **public corporations** (**nationalised industries**) and situations where local government sells services.

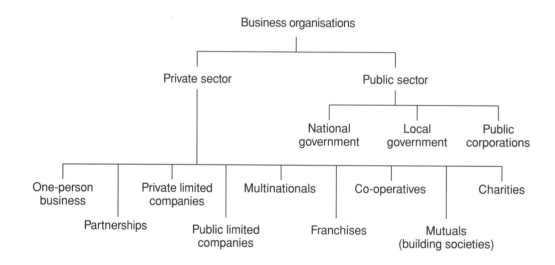

It is important that you understand the concept of **limited liability**. This means that **shareholders** are only risking the money they paid or owe for shares. On the other hand, at least one partner in a partnership and a **sole trader** will have unlimited liability. They are risking all their wealth. If the business goes **bankrupt** they are liable for (have to pay) all the debts, even if this means selling their own home.

It is easy to see the attraction of becoming a private limited company (**ltd**). Another major advantage is having access to much larger sources of funds.

Public limited companies (**plcs**) have even greater access to funds through the **Stock Exchange**. However, there are disadvantages to **going public**. The disclosure requirements are much greater. The possibility of mergers and **takeovers** is much greater. The value of the company may be subject to the fluctuations of the stock market as opposed to its own performance. For these reasons, amongst others, there have been examples in recent years of famous companies reverting to private status, e.g. Richard Branson's Virgin Group and Andrew Lloyd Webber's Really Useful Group.

Many of the high-street companies with which you are familiar, e.g. Marks and Spencer plc and Barclays Bank plc, are not just plc's but also multinationals. That is, they have bases in more than one country. You should know the reasons for this and the implications for the company and the countries involved.

Franchises have become very popular recently and have an excellent record of success compared to other business start-ups. A franchise is the right to use a business idea or format. It is purchased by a **franchisee** from the owner of the idea, the **franchisor**. The extent to which these rights can be exercised will be determined by the **franchise agreement**. These agreements vary extensively in terms of how detailed, constricting and expensive they are.

Many workers have set up businesses which are owned by the workers, run on democratic lines and where no single person can own more of the business than any other. These are known as **worker cooperatives**. You should be familiar with **consumer cooperatives** through the 'Co-op'.

You should know the arguments for and against **state ownership** of industry.

Industries can also be classified according to the kind of product/service they provide and their direct use or not of raw materials.

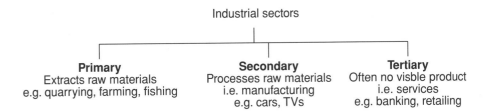

Industrial sectors

Primary
Extracts raw materials
e.g. quarrying, farming, fishing

Secondary
Processes raw materials
i.e. manufacturing
e.g. cars, TVs

Tertiary
Often no visble product
i.e. services
e.g. banking, retailing

1 Business organisations

1 Define the term 'multinational company'. (2)

AEB

2 Under the Partnership Act how would the profits of a partnership be divided between three partners if a formal agreement did not exist? (2)

AEB

3 What is a public corporation? Give an example. (3)

AEB

4 List **two** factors that distinguish a private limited company from a public limited company. (2)

AEB

5 Read the extract and answer the questions that follow.

New power to innovators

When Rhone-Poulenc, the French chemical giant, decided to break into plant biotechnology in 1984, it used a new form of strategic partnership with a small business to gain access to the latest technology.

The company decided to invest £1m in Calgene, a small American biotechnology business, which was sliding into debt. In return for being bailed out, Calgene undertook a research-and-development project for Rhone-Poulenc. It granted the large company world marketing rights for products resulting from the project, providing it received royalties.

By 1987 Calgene had made a spectacular recovery and Rhone-Poulenc was successfully involved in plant biotechnology. Calgene went public at $14 a share, giving Rhone-Poulenc nearly a tenfold increase in its investment.

This partnership was made possible by corporate venturing, a strategy that is just beginning to take hold in Britain and elsewhere in Europe.

An advisor on corporate venturing, Anthony Lunch, says 'It can be enormously difficult for entrepreneurial businesses to be accepted as suppliers when they have nothing to show other than clever product development and enthusiastic management. Having a larger company as a significant shareholder is a powerful means of opening the door to larger contracts and overseas opportunities.'

MediSense, a young biotechnology company based in Abingdon, Berkshire, has used a corporate partnership to penetrate the competitive American market.

Three years ago it joined with Baxter Healthcare, a big American company in this field. Baxter supplied $25m in debt and equity, giving it a 20% share in MediSense. In return, the American company has the right of refusal to be the exclusive distributor of up to 50 products developed by MediSense.

MediSense's partnership with the Americans has helped it to attract around $3m from venture-capital funds. 'We were immediately attracted to the company by the strength of its marketing arrangements with Baxter Healthcare', says David Hough of Royal Life Insurance, one of MediSense's new investors.

Many strategy experts believe that such joint alliances will become more popular as companies seek to diversify.

Source: Adapted from an article by Marion Devine in *The Sunday Times*, 14 August 1988

(a) (i) Explain the term 'corporate venturing'. (4)

(ii) Why might firms prefer a 'corporate venture' to a merger? (4)

(b) What benefits might be brought to the corporate partnership by:

(i) the small business; (4)

(ii) the large business? (4)

(c) Suggest possible problems that might arise from a 'corporate venture'. (4)

AEB

6 Study the information and answer the questions that follow.

The universe of franchising

The franchising business has mushroomed during the past decade. Not only have numbers of franchisors multiplied, the number of franchisees per franchise has also increased.

A clear indication of the health of franchising compared to the generality of small businesses appears in a survey undertaken for the *Financial Times* in 1986. Within a five-year period, 80% of all new small businesses had ceased trading, for one reason or another. By contrast, well over 80% of franchised businesses were still trading after a five-year period. However, the more recent Power Report also notes an increase in the failure rate of both franchised systems and of individual franchised outlets, although these come out at a modest 14% and 10% respectively. Problems, it observes, stem not only from the franchises themselves, but from failures of other kinds, in selling and basic business and marketing skills.

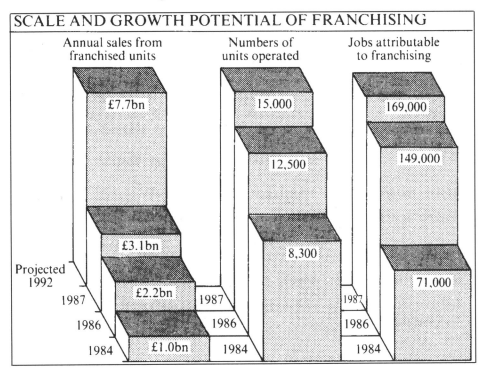

SCALE AND GROWTH POTENTIAL OF FRANCHISING

Annual sales from franchised units: £7.7bn, £3.1bn, £2.2bn, £1.0bn

Numbers of units operated: 15,000, 12,500, 8,300

Jobs attributable to franchising: 169,000, 149,000, 71,000

Projected 1992, 1987, 1986, 1984

Source: Adapted from an article by Derek Ayling, *Management Today*, April 1988
(Diagram – Power Research Associates)

(a) Explain the term 'franchising'. (4)

(b) (i) Calculate the percentage change between 1986 and 1987 of each of sales from franchised units, units operated and jobs attributable to franchising. (4)

   (ii) What do your figures suggest about developments in franchising between 1986 and 1987? (5)

(c) (i) Explain the advantages to a business of selling franchises. (6)

   (ii) Explain the advantages of starting a business by buying a franchise. (6)

AEB

1 Business organisations

7 Multinational companies offer a number of attractions to developing countries, and yet they are often viewed by these countries with great suspicion. Outline the potential benefits and drawbacks for such countries.

(25)

AEB

8 Study the information and answer the questions that follow.

Systech Limited

Michael Rowe and Oliver Vetty were children of the computer revolution. Although they came from different parts of the country their school careers were almost identical. They were both clever mathematicians, and they both had an almost obsessive interest in computers and computer applications. This tended to make their conversation rather uninteresting to many of their contemporaries and in consequence earned them few friends. At their Universities this pattern remained unchanged and they gained reputations for being 'loners', seemingly preferring the company of machines to that of their fellow undergraduates.

They met when they started to work for Megasystems Ltd., an American multinational which produced computer software for large, corporate clients. The two immediately recognised their personal compatibility, and soon formed a technically brilliant team, which earned them rapid promotion.

After a few years Mike and Oliver identified a gap in the systems market. Large corporate clients were well serviced by companies such as Megasystems Ltd., while small companies tended to buy software 'off the shelf'. Medium sized organisations were left with little support, and it was to them that the two friends looked for work. They formed a company, Systech Ltd., and started work from a spare room in Oliver's house near Reading.

Their initial reading of the market proved correct, and, given their contacts within the computer industry, they soon had more than enough work which generated profits large enough to keep their borrowing down to an absolute minimum. Indeed, after less than two years they realised that they would need more people. Of course from the beginning they had had to employ freelance programmers and temporary secretaries, but this was proving both expensive and inefficient, and so in 1986 they took on a full time software engineer, a programmer, and a secretary. Clearly their accommodation was inadequate and so they moved into a purpose-built office close to the M4 motorway. They negotiated a five year lease, paying £1,000 per month for the first year, rising by 10% per year until 1990 when the lease would be re-negotiated.

Clearly these changes for Mike and Oliver were quite fundamental, but the partners continued to concentrate on that side of the business which fascinated them, but which tended to isolate them from the rest of the staff. Given their backgrounds, this did not worry them; indeed to them it was very familiar, and almost comforting.

By September 1988 the company was at a crossroads. In January of that year a marketing specialist, Anna Logge, had been employed to counter the growing competition in Systech's market segment. Anna took the job partly as a new challenge, partly because of the attractive salary package she was offered, but also because she was impressed by Mike and Oliver's management style. They appeared to be willing to allow her almost total freedom of action and decision-making within the marketing area.

Given this freedom, Anna was highly successful in negotiating a large contract with a local authority, the Borough of Eastminster. The Borough had privatised a large number of its services, and it needed a sophisticated systems package to administer the new arrangements.

Apart from the obvious financial appeal of this new contract it also offered Systech considerable possibilities for the future. If the system proved to be efficient, it could become the basis for similar work with other local authorities. Unfortunately the contract required successful installation by the end of 1989, and its acceptance would have an impact upon the direction of the whole company. The decision to take the Eastminster contract was made by Mike and Oliver while they were on holiday that September visiting a computer exhibition in Birmingham.

One immediate impact was the apparent need to change the company's premises once again, this time to a Science Park close to Newbury College of Technology. The rent on these prestigious premises was £40,000 per year, but the decision appeared to pay off immediately when the company recruited a post-graduate research programmer from the College. The company's administration staff had by now risen to three.

1989 was naturally dominated by the Eastminster contract, and when Oliver received a letter of dissatisfaction from Lockeye Mouldings Ltd about the level of service it was receiving, he was not too concerned. He did write a letter apologising, but he didn't speak directly to the managing director, who was a rather blunt Midlander, because he tended to get embarrassed and flustered in such circumstances and, if anything, tended to make things worse rather than better. He should perhaps have given the task to his marketing director, Anna, but with the demands on his technical knowledge and expertise, he just couldn't find the time. In the event the incident didn't seem that significant because the Eastminster system was installed on time, and the company received a letter of commendation and recommendation from the council written by its influential leader Lady Graveswell.

In fact the Lockeye complaint was important. In January 1990 Lockeye terminated their contract with Systech, and six months later another major customer did the same, again citing poor service. Anna resigned immediately, saying that she had never been informed about these problems; that there was more to marketing than just selling; and that she felt like she was little more than a two-bit player in the organisation – certainly not a director.

Just to add to Systech's worries, the economy was plunging into recession. A retail customer withdrew from a proposed deal, and local authorities, far from beating a path to Systech's door, were finding that their finances were in disarray given uncertainties with local authority finance. Consequently they could not afford new systems. Finally, in June 1991, GO-2-IT Carriers Ltd went out of business, still owing Systech £2,000.

(a) What are **either** the strengths **or** the weaknesses of Mike and Oliver as managers? Support your answer with references to the case study as well as to your theoretical understanding of management. (10)

(b) (i) Give the ratios for:
- Net profit margin;
- Gearing. (2)

(ii) Calculate the net profit margin as a percentage for Systech Ltd for the years 1985, 1986 and 1987, using the **Appendices** on the next page. (2)

(iii) Would you expect the gearing ratio to be low or high for Systech Ltd during these years? **Briefly** explain your answer. (2)

(c) (i) Using all the data in the case study and the appendices, identify and explain which you consider to be the critical points in the development of Systech Ltd. (10)

(ii) To what extent do these critical points explain Systech's present condition? (7)

(iii) What other important factors are there? Explain your answer. (7)

(d) Systech Ltd exhibits many of the difficulties faced by a small firm. Using the case study where appropriate, explain the steps which can be taken to minimise such difficulties. (10)

AEB

Appendix 1: Systech Ltd – Contract revenues, costs and profits information

	1985	1986	1987	1988	1989	1990	1991
Contract revenue	£	£	£	£	£	£	£
Lockeye Mouldings Ltd	80,000	7,000	7,000	7,000	7,000		
Homecare DIY Stores	60,000	6,500	6,500	6,500	6,500	6,500	
Nowax Ltd		70,000	6,500	6,500	6,500	6,500	6,500
Fishers Foundry		65,000	6,500	6,500	6,500	6,500	6,500
Greenacres Gardens			70,000	7,000	7,000	7,000	7,000
Opticon UK Ltd			75,000	7,500	7,500	7,500	7,500
Happidog Petfood				90,000	9,000	9,000	9,000
Wheelers Biscuits				50,000	45,000	6,000	6,000
Eastminster					80,000	80,000	
GO-2-IT Carriers Ltd						30,000	20,000
Total revenue	140,000	148,500	171,500	181,000	175,000	159,000	62,500
Costs							
Administration costs	7,000	7,425	8,575	9,050	8,750	7,950	3,125
Salaries	35,000	52,000	55,000	85,000	95,000	100,000	110,000
Premises	2,000	12,000	13,200	14,520	40,000	42,000	44,000
Total costs	44,000	71,425	76,775	108,570	143,750	149,950	157,125
Operating profit	**96,000**	**77,075**	**94,725**	**72,430**	**31,250**	**9,050**	**–94,625**

Appendix 2: Systech Ltd – Revenues, costs and profits

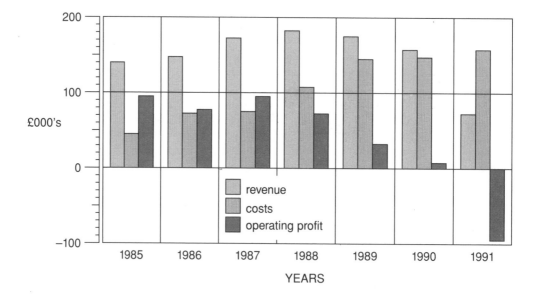

Marketing is a very popular topic – dangerously popular. Far too many students answer examination questions by writing everything they know about marketing rather than by applying their knowledge. If you use this 'scatter-gun' approach of just rewriting notes, you gain only low-level knowledge marks rather than the high marks associated with analysis and evaluation. This is sad, because it is likely that you enjoy this topic, know it well and therefore write quite good notes and finish the question thinking that you have done well. In fact you will almost certainly have failed it, when you were capable of passing if you had used your skills and knowledge to answer the question set.

Marketing can be defined as identifying and meeting consumers' wants profitably. It is not just selling, but the whole process of researching customer needs, designing the product, promoting the product, getting it into the hands of the consumer and ensuring that the cost of doing all this is less than the revenue.

Customer wants are identified through **market research**. There are two main classifications of research: **desk research** and **field research**. Desk research is cheaper because it uses published material, perhaps already available in the firm, in trade magazines, in government statistics or from some other source. However, because it has been produced for some other purpose it may not provide the information a firm needs. Field research can be specifically commissioned, and therefore targeted to provide detailed information. An example of field research would be a consumer panel testing and commenting on a trial version of a product.

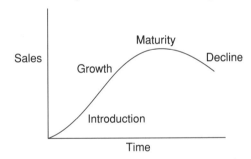

Market research is the first stage of the **product life cycle** (see diagram above). Products go through various stages from introduction to growth to maturity and finally into decline. The length of time it takes a product to go through each stage varies. Some high-fashion products are designed to go through all the stages in just one season. Other products, for example cabbages, have been in the maturity stage for centuries. The vast majority of ideas which firms come up with never get out of the development stage. This is because firms have decided either that there is no market for them or that they cannot satisfy the market profitably. The early stages of the product life cycle are expensive: paying for research, prototypes and machines, training workers, advertising, etc., while at the same time the product is not generating any revenue. During the introduction stage sales will hopefully take off, but marketing will still be expensive and production costs will always be incurred. Even for successful products it will be some time before the cash flowing in will match all the cash which is flowing out and that which has been paid out on research and development. The diagram below shows the typical relationship between profits and sales.

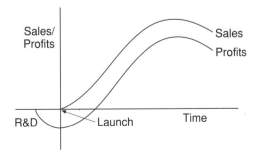

REVISION SUMMARY

A firm would be in a much safer position if it had a range of products at different stages of the product life cycle. This is called a product **portfolio**. The Boston Consulting Group has identified a classification of products called the **Boston matrix**. When a product is approaching the decline phase, the firm can either decide to end production or to try to revitalise the market. The second approach is known as an **extension strategy**.

How the product or service is marketed will in part depend on the stage in the cycle it has reached. It will also depend on a range of other factors, e.g. the product itself, the competition, the state of the economy, the size of the firm, etc. Four main factors are identified in most textbooks, known as the **4P's**. They are **price**, **promotion**, **place** and **product**. A firm must ensure that it pays attention to each of the 4P's and ensures that they are consistent with each other.

Firms can adopt a variety of **pricing strategies** depending on the **constraints** it faces. If the firm is a large monopoly producer facing no potential competitors and making a high-status, well established product it may be able to charge high prices and make **super normal profits**. The absence of any of these conditions may change the strategy. A small firm facing many competitors may have to charge low **competitive** prices set by the market or follow the prices set by the **market leader**. If a firm introduces a new innovative product it may choose to charge a high price, hoping that consumers who like to be seen to be the first to buy a product will be prepared to pay the price. This is known as **skim pricing** because the firm is skimming the 'cream' off the market before competitors inevitably enter the market. These competitors, in order to attract customers away from the innovative firm, will probably charge lower prices. This is known as **penetration pricing**.

Promotion, like marketing, is much more than just **selling**. Some products are sold door-to-door by sales representatives, e.g. Avon. Some are sold by holding parties, e.g. Tupperware. Fast-moving consumer goods or **FMCG's**, e.g. baked beans, make extensive use of **brand names** which are then advertised on television, in magazines, on billboards, etc. Marks and Spencer do not use television advertising at all, but put immense effort into **merchandising** and **point-of-sale** techniques. A wide variety of promotional techniques could be used depending on the firm's promotional budget and the type of product. An engineering firm selling a specialist machine will use very different techniques from the local corner shop.

One element of promotion is so important that some textbooks classify it as a fifth **P**, i.e. **packaging**. Packaging is vital in protecting some products, but for many its main role is to attract customers. This is important whatever combination of promotional techniques a firm uses, but it is crucial that customers actually buy the product. This is neatly summed up by the mnemonic **AIDA**, which stands for 'attention, interest, desire, and action'. An award-winning advertising campaign that excites the first three but does not lead to increased sales is a costly waste of money.

If you need to revise this subject more thoroughly, see the relevant topics in the *Letts* A level *Business Studies Study Guide*.

There is no point in producing an excellent reasonably priced product if it is not available at the right time in the right **place** to suit the consumer. Some products will be sold in shops such as Harrods, and others in shops such as Kwik-Save. 'Place' is the term used to cover physical distribution, i.e. transport, but in this context it is more importantly the **channel of distribution**. This refers to the use or lack of use of **wholesalers**, **retailers**, **agents**, **mail-order**, etc.

The 'product' must meet the wants of the consumers, even if these wants have been created in the mind of the consumer by the firm's promotional techniques. In the past many firms were product oriented, i.e. they thought of the product first and then expected customers to buy, even if it was not quite right or at a price they were prepared to pay or sold in a convenient place. More and more firms now are **market oriented**. They identify the market first and the price consumers are prepared to pay. Through their research they balance the 4P's and, most importantly, work out if they can make the product at a profit. The product must carry out the tasks the consumers want, will probably be pleasing on the eye and should be relatively easy to produce.

1 (a) How might the marketing operations of a product-oriented firm differ from those of a market-oriented firm?

 (b) Using any organisation with which you are familiar, explain how the operations of the marketing department and the accounts department might interact and interrelate. (8)

NEAB

2 (a) What factors might influence how the demand for a product reacts to a change in its price or in the price of another item?

 (b) How might the imposition of VAT on books affect your demand? (8)

NEAB

3 Read the extract and answer the questions that follow.

After 31 years the Mini keeps on growing

The French adore them and the Japanese simply cannot get enough. After 31 years in production, the evergreen Mini has
5 become one of Britain's biggest export earners.

Rover yesterday disclosed that output of the little car is at its highest for five years with 1,000
10 rolling off the assembly lines at the company's Longbridge plant, in Birmingham, every week.

Most of the demand is coming from abroad where the Mini has
15 become a cult car. It is the best-selling imported car in Japan, with more than 10,400 sold there this year.

Rover sales staff, sensing a
20 trend, pandered to the demand by introducing a new version of the Mini Cooper, the rally car which enjoyed huge success in the 1960s. Now the Cooper accounts for four
25 out of ten of worldwide sales of Minis and the car is commanding premium prices when the rest of the market is having to discount.

The enormous success of the Mini after more than three 30 decades is baffling Rover executives, who were going to axe the model six years ago. But Sir Graham Day decided to keep the car running when he took over as 35 chairman in 1986 because, he said, it was a 'nice little earner'. How much the Mini is earning has not been revealed by Rover, but export sales could be worth about 40 £180 million, according to industry estimates.

Rover said: 'Foreign markets love the Mini. In France, women love the car with special paint jobs 45 as a chic runabout. That is why the Mini Cooper is so popular.'

Its original design is little changed, although its engine has been cleaned up to meet modern 50 environmental emission laws. More than five million have now been built and the Mini sits alongside the Volkswagen Beetle and Citroën 2CV as one of the 55 most readily identifiable cars in the world.

Source: Adapted from *The Times*, 22nd December, 1990

 (a) What proportion of total Mini production is sold in Japan? (2)

 (b) Explain why 'the car is commanding premium prices when the rest of the market is having to discount' (lines 26–28). (6)

 (c) Identify and discuss the product extension strategies that resulted in the growth in sales of the Mini. (8)

 (d) What **two** methods might a government use to protect the car industry from foreign competition? (4)

(e) What financial justification could Sir Graham Day have had for reversing the decision to take the car out of production? (5)

AEB

4 'When selling a good, price is the single most important factor.' Evaluate this statement. (25)

AEB

5 Read the extract and answer the questions which follow.

Mineral waters in the UK

1   During the 1970's, Perrier (UK) built the market almost single handed, aided by the 'Eau so successful' advertising campaign. By the early 80's, there were five major competitors each contributing to spending on advertising and stimulating market growth. In 1983, there was a major marketing windfall – a national water strike –

5   which caused the market to leap by almost 50% in one year. At the same time, the market began to segment on a price basis, as the premium brands gained national distribution through grocery outlets and own labels were introduced.

The UK Mineral Water Market
(Million litres)

1980	25
1982	34
1984	65
1986	105
1987	150
1990 (Estimate)	210

Source: *Perrier UK estimates*

Today, the ownership of the mineral water brands can be divided between those companies which have a diversified product range, e.g. Nestlé, Cadbury Schweppes,

10 and those who are purely mineral water producers (e.g. Perrier, Highland Spring).

Whilst product life-cycle theory suggests that volume growth will inevitably slow down, the Chief Executive Officer of Perrier (UK) estimates that the average Briton will be drinking ten litres of bottled water a year within two decades (*Financial Times*, 1986). A British Market Research Bureau (1986) survey showed that 34% of UK

15 adults claimed to drink bottled mineral water. 25% of these claimed to drink it once a month or more.

The UK consumer and derived brand benefits
Forty-one per cent of UK mineral water is consumed by Londoners, perhaps due to the fact that the original 'eau' campaign was targeted upon 'image-conscious trendies' who saw mineral water as a status symbol.

20   As the distribution base broadens (56% of national sales are now distributed through major multiples – Mintel Market Intelligence, 1988) and the market structure changes, it seems likely that with increasing consumer demand, a mass market will develop from the niche position previously occupied.

There is considerable evidence to suggest that other environmental and social

25 factors are also encouraging these structural changes.

(Source: *The Quarterly Review of Marketing – Summer 1989*)

(a) What factors might affect a grocery outlet's decision to introduce 'own label' products? (5)

(b) Assume that total advertising expenditure in the UK Mineral Water Industry was £2m in 1986 and £2.5m in 1987. If other factors remain the same, calculate the advertising elasticity of demand for the UK Mineral Water Market between 1986 and 1987, and comment on the significance of the result. (5)

(c) How might those 'who saw mineral water as a status symbol' (line 19) have been targeted by the marketing department? (4)

(d) How might marketing strategies change as the distribution broadens and the market structure changes to a mass market from a 'niche position' in the market (lines 22–23)? (3)

(e) What factors other than marketing might have led to the increase in sales of mineral water? (3)

AEB

3 *People in organisations*

People are vital for all organisations. They make the difference between success and failure. Large firms will employ personnel specialists. In a one-person business the owner will, amongst their many other roles, be looking after the welfare and motivation of their employees.

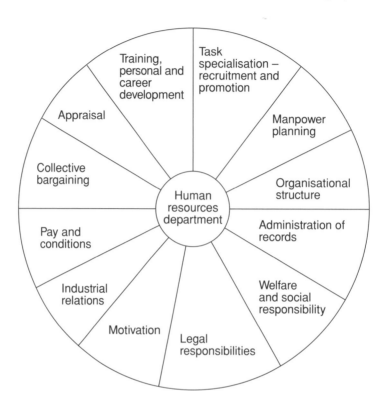

The personnel department has many functions. **Communications** will be a major feature, as will advising management on **organisational structure**. **Manpower planning** ensures that the organisation has the right number of people with appropriate skills. The firm's **training**, **induction** and **appraisal** systems will address the skills of current employees. There may also be a need to employ new workers. This will involve **recruitment** and **selection**, where the personnel department will advise other departments on the appropriate methods and legal requirements. It may also involve reducing the size of the organisation. There are legal procedures to follow when making staff **redundant**. An individual member of staff may lose their job for other reasons, e.g. inability to do the job or fighting at work. The personnel department would deal with these matters under the firm's **capability and disciplinary procedures**. If there are **trade union** members employed by the firm there will be negotiations with their representatives. Maintaining good **industrial relations** will be an important function. A major aspect of this will be negotiations over **pay and conditions**. Workers will want the best wages/salaries they can obtain, and firms wish to produce as efficiently as possible. Workers will want, amongst other things, good holidays, reasonable hours and as decent and safe a working environment as possible. Firms will vary in their response. Some firms will seek, within the law, to give away as little as possible. Others believe that if they treat their workforce well they will gain so much in productivity that their average costs will be lower than in other firms.

This leads neatly to the other major feature of this part of the syllabus: **Motivation Theory**. There are many different theories on what motivates people, some of which are diametrically opposed. You will need to learn the ideas of several different management 'gurus' and how to apply them to unfamiliar situations. You also need to be aware that there are no right answers, and that these ideas go in and out of fashion as rapidly as clothing styles. The theories tend to be classified into two opposing camps. On the one hand, the **Classical** or **Scientific Management**

School, and on the other the **Human Relations School**. **Douglas McGregor** illustrated the opposing views in his **Theory X** and **Theory Y**, though it should be noted that some people think this puts the scientific management school in an unfair light. Theory X has a very negative attitude to workers and states that they are naturally lazy, self-centred and hedonistic. Therefore the appropriate management style to adopt is **autocratic**, forcing workers to work by a system of rewards and punishments. Workers will not be trusted and their work will be constantly supervised and checked. Theory Y has a positive view of human nature. Workers naturally enjoy their work and will try to do their best. They like to take the initiative in their work and welcome responsibility. They are motivated by the work itself, rather than by money. If this theory is right, the appropriate management style to adopt is **democratic**. Workers should be involved in decision making. Their ideas should be encouraged. There is no need to have many layers of management and supervision. Managers can trust their workers and **delegate** important tasks.

In the 1990s, some managers have adopted all aspects of one theory, while others adopt a mixture of the two. Recently, the so-called **Japanese management** style (many of the ideas of which are based on the work of an American called Deming) has become popular. Many firms are removing the distinction between staff and workers. They are making use of **quality circles** and other **total quality management** techniques.

REVISION SUMMARY

If you need to revise this subject more thoroughly, see the relevant topics in the *Letts* **A level Business Studies Study Guide.**

3 *People in organisations*

1 With reference to a firm or firms of which you have direct knowledge, outline critically **three** of the following:

   (a) **either** recruitment procedures **or** induction training.

   (b) ways in which personnel have had to adapt to change.

   (c) the impact of Health and Safety at Work law.

   (d) non-financial attempts to motivate staff.

   (e) the barriers to effective workplace communication.

   (15)

   UCLES

2 The table below shows UK activity rates for women in selected years. The figures indicate the percentage of women in the workforce aged 16 to 60 years (inclusive).

	1971	1976	1981	1986	1990
%	43.9	46.8	47.6	49.6	52.8

Source: *Social Trends*

   (a) Give reasons for the trend in the activity rates for women as shown in the table.   (4)

   (b) Since women make up some 47% of the UK's workforce, why do you think there are so few women in senior managerial positions?   (4)

   (c) Women tend to be under-represented in trade unions. Why might this be the case?   (4)

   (d) Why is it that average female earnings are approximately 70% of average male earnings?

   (4)

   NEAB

3 Read the following extracts adapted from *Quality Circles in Action* by M. Robson and answer the questions below.

   1   'Though Quality Circles first developed in Japan during the late 1950s and early 1960s, the approach is based on Western theories of management, notably Douglas McGregor's Theory Y . . .'
       'Firstly Quality Circles is an approach which allows people to become more involved, but
   5   puts no pressure on them to do so; in other words the approach is entirely voluntary at all levels of the organisation . . .'
       'Secondly people who join in are encouraged to solve their own job-related problems . . .'
       'Thirdly members solve their problems in an organised way; in other words they are given training in the skills of systematic problem solving and of working together effectively in a
   10 group . . .'
       'A Quality Circle consists of a group of 4 to 10 volunteers who work for the same first-line supervisor and who meet regularly to identify, analyse and solve their work problems . . .'
       '. . . the group does not need to consist of the entire workforce from that section'; only those that volunteer.
   15 '. . . the group meets regularly once a week, for an hour and in paid time . . .'
       '. . . the groups at their meetings do not stop at the identification of problems for passing on to management for solution, they utilise the training they receive to analyse and solve them and then present their own findings to management . . .'
       '. . . there are 3 main possible goals: staff involvement, people development and the
   20 generation of tangible benefits . . .' for the organisation and the people in it.

(a) As the Training Manager for Alpha Components Ltd., write a report to the Managing Director, outlining **four** possible benefits for the company of introducing Quality Circles. (10)

(b) Consider and explain **five** problems the company might encounter in establishing and operating Quality Circles. (10)

(c) What evidence is there to suggest that 'Quality Circles' is based on McGregor's Theory Y (lines 2–3)? (5)

AEB

4 Ingersoll Engineers, a management consultancy, have produced the following information from a survey into the use and effectiveness of eight different communication methods between managers and staff.

Study the data and answer the questions which follow.

Communication Methods
(Between managers and staff)

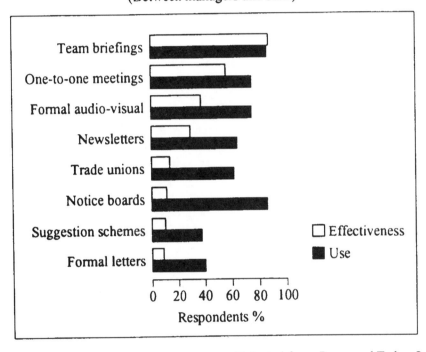

(Adapted from *Personnel Today*, January 1993)

(a) From the data above, identify the **two** most frequently used methods of communication. (2)

(b) Outline **three** reasons why notice boards are a less effective communication method than team briefings and one-to-one meetings. (6)

(c) Discuss **three** ways in which *effective* communication methods may affect staff morale in a company. (6)

(d) Examine **two** possible reasons why a firm might continue to use communication methods that are less effective rather than concentrate on the more effective methods. (6)

AEB

5 Read the following case study passages carefully and then answer the questions that follow.

A
Euro Disney loses visitors – and £30m

The Walt Disney group, which yesterday reported a 28 per cent rise in profits for the year to September, will postpone taking its share of income from Euro Disney for this year and next following the revelation of heavy losses at its new Paris-based theme park.

Euro Disney unveiled a loss of Fr188 million (£30 million) after 172 days in business compared with predictions of a Fr204 million profit for its first year.

Although chairman Robert Fitzpatrick declared himself 'pleased' with the outcome, the official statement accompanying the Euro Disney figures detailed a catalogue of adverse conditions which had affected performances at the theme park. The company also admitted that a profit is unlikely for 1993.

Attendance figures at 6.8 million, although ahead of anything achieved in the early days of other Disney theme parks, fell below expectations. And, with the bleaker winter weather, visitors have continued to tail off in October and November – to as low as 3,000 on one day last week compared with the park's 30,000 capacity.

Hotel occupancy rates, at 74 per cent, were lower than anticipated and Euro Disney also admitted that, once inside the complex, visitors had spent less than had been hoped. High French interest rates increased finance charges and falling property prices hit development plans.

Analysts at Paribas Capital Markets said they saw no reason to revise their forecasts of a loss of Fr210 million for next year – a figure which includes Fr147 million of 'dividend' to the Walt Disney parent group.

They pointed out that yesterday's figures benefited from a one-off tax credit and also expressed concern over the failure of Euro Disney to provide for the 1992 dividend payment of Fr113 million.

Although Walt Disney, which owns 49 per cent of Euro Disney, has said it will defer taking its management fee of 3 per cent of revenues for this year and next, there is no question of these payments being waived entirely. They will be made from 1994 onwards, dependent on the level of profits achieved, but will not rise above 25 per cent of the total surplus.

Mr Fitzpatrick admitted yesterday that greater efforts had to be made to attract visitors during the low season. Operating costs and discretionary spending will also be targeted.

But following an initial investment of Fr24 billion, Euro Disney has high fixed costs about which it can do very little and it is also concerned about the outlook for tourism in recession hit Europe.

[From an article by Lisa Buckingham in *The Guardian*, 20/11/92]

B

Disney takes white-knuckle ride as the cash fails to flow

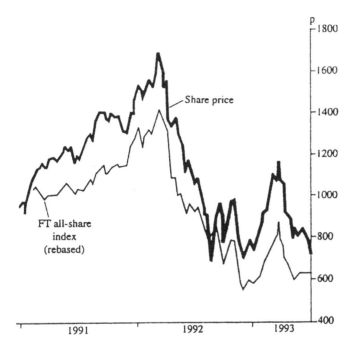

Euro Disneyland, the theme park east of Paris, has put on hold plans to build a Fr9 billion second site after a disastrous trading statement that concedes the park will fail to make a profit even in the potentially lucrative summer months of this year.

The shares plummeted 108p to 675p on news from the company that a loss of Fr500 million would be incurred in the third quarter to end-June. Analysts had been hoping for a break-even position.

Euro Disney also said it expected to lose money in the fourth quarter, covering the summer months when attendance is at its highest. The company is drawing up 'a thorough review of its financial structure and its development strategy'.

This is unlikely to be completed before next spring. Until then, the Walt Disney Company, which has a half share in the development, 'has agreed to help finance the company's capital expansion and working capital requirement', a statement read.

Philippe Bourguignon, president directeur general of Euro Disney, said the current economic environment did not allow the company to proceed with the development of a second theme park.

The third-quarter loss was blamed on lower than expected visitor spending on food and merchandise in the theme park and at the surrounding hotels.

Analysts are braced for losses in the summer of perhaps Fr200 million. The tourist industry in France has been badly hit by the recession and the fall in the value of sterling, the lira and the peseta which discouraged visitors. Plans for raising revenue from real estate development were scuppered by the depressed Paris real estate market.

The immediate effect has been a delay for an unspecified period in the building of the second theme park, initially due to open in 1995.

More significant is the decision to review the project's finances in a bid to make it profitable. Sources close to the company were stressing that any option would be considered, although they backed off from speculation that the American joint owner might walk away from its equity, perhaps by selling it on.

This would leave the corporation earning lucrative management fees from running the park and hotels as well as profits from the plethora of Disney merchandise.

A less radical solution would be a rights issue to wipe out debts that would take years to erode from pure cash flow.

Other alternatives are sales of assets such as the hotels or a general restructuring of the package of debts incurred when the £3 billion park was built.

Euro Disney opened with a $10 million party but ran straight into flak from its French hosts. One intellectual described it as a 'cultural Chernobyl'.

The first annual figures last November revealed a net loss of Fr188 million and a token dividend payment. The park has consistently failed to meet ambitious attendance forecasts drawn up before the recession reined in consumer spending. The Magic Kingdom is open and Mickey is at the door to greet visitors. But many have been too strapped for cash to enjoy the experience.

[*The Times*, 9/7/93]

C
Castles in Cold Air

Euro Disney needs several transformation scenes

Any mirror on the wall, however, could have foreseen Snow White's troubles at Marne-la-Vallée. Paris may look a central location on a planning map; but whereas Americans think nothing of a weekend flight or a 15-hour drive to Orlando, the people of Dresden, Oslo and Athens see Euro Disney as several countries and a very expensive plane journey away.

The Disney executives should have first tried standing in an empty parking lot on a November afternoon or queuing for an hour and a half with three children to spend fifty seconds on Indiana Jones et le Temple du Peril. Those who rejected Spain because of its peripheral position forgot its weather.

Even a cliched understanding of French likes and habits should have made it obvious that a day out with no alcohol and no proper restaurants is hardly a Frenchman's idea of fun. American planners – and their French partners – should also have looked at the relative attractions of Orlando and Paris. Whereas Disney World ranks as one of the most vibrant attractions in Florida, tourists are not drawn to Paris by the magnetism of Euro Disney: there is much else to do.

The Magic Kingdom has not been well managed. As well as the rain and the surly staff, there are the prices. The franc is strong, and Euro Disney is too expensive: for many, it is cheaper to fly to Florida. No one wants to pay £60 for a Mickey Mouse doll. Few wanted the package rate at the hotels even after recent price cuts. The park borrowed too much money and banked on recouping too much of it from ancillary services. In order to survive, the Magic Kingdom may have to become a French national treasure. Pass the magic wand.

[*The Guardian*, October 93]

D
Euro Disney future in doubt

Euro Disney executives are this weekend clustered in crisis talks with Walt Disney, the group's parent, over the future of the beleaguered French leisure park. Among the options on the table are an injection of new funds, a rights issue or even potential closure. Nothing, according to Disney sources, has been ruled out.

A spokesman stressed: 'There are no sacred cows', adding: 'They are taking it back to the drawing board and reassessing the financing. We will go off and examine everything, a rights issue, or closing it'. Last week the company released disappointing sales figures showing a 15% decline in revenues to £166m for the third quarter to June. Spring is supposed to be one of the park's busiest times. The company is also on course to report a full-year loss of £200m.

The news prompted one leading analyst to say: 'This company is bust. It can't survive without a major capital injection.'

One of the key issues is the high cost base. The spokesman confirmed: 'They're stripping it right down'. The company has cut staff from almost 19,000 at the end of July last year to less than 16,000. The results of the restructuring will be made known next year.

The full extent of Euro Disney's problems became apparent when it was unable to proceed with a second phase of the park, close to the first one, earlier this year.

It now finds itself in the awkward situation of needing visitors to the second park to boost flagging hotel attendances in the first park and increase revenues, but does not have the cash for the second phase.

Initially Euro Disney expected to be profitable in its first year, but it has been hit by the European recession. The French were lukewarm towards the concept from the outset and the strength of the French franc has deterred many foreigners, particularly the British.

However, the company admits its biggest problem is that even when attendances are high, visitors are not spending enough. 'The real issue is that the attendance figures are there, but the company is still not making money', said a spokesman.

Euro Disney recently announced it had asked Walt Disney for financial support while it tried to restructure its debt. The Euro Disney spokesman said the parent company was supportive: 'They are making pots of money. Euro Disney is just a small part of the group'.

He stressed that Walt Disney considered Euro Disney a long-term commitment claiming: 'For them a short-term project is 10 years'.

But persistent rumours suggest Walt Disney is losing patience with Euro Disney, which is limiting profits at the parent. The shares rose 55p last week, before closing at 735p on the hope that the company would benefit from lower French interest rates.

[From an article by Helen Davidson in *The Sunday Times*, 15/8/93]

E

One out of ten jobs to go at Euro Disneyland

Almost one employee in ten is to be trimmed from the workforce of Euro Disneyland, the theme park a few miles east of Paris that has been dogged by low attendance levels since it opened 18 months ago.

The torrential rain of recent weeks has been the latest of many blows suffered by the park. Now Euro Disney, which says the cuts are not connected with any lack of visitors but concedes they are linked to the state of the French economy, has started the lengthy consultation procedure required under French law before the 950 jobs, all among administrative and management staff, can be cut from the 11,100 strong workforce.

The move comes just months after the company deferred any decision on whether to proceed with the ambitious second phase of the development in the light of poor performance from the park. The company says the job losses are inevitable 'now that Euro Disney is completing its transition from a start-up organisation to a full operating company'. They are, therefore, concentrated on those employees connected with the start-up of the scheme and its initial financing.

In July, the management started a strategic review of the business, which has to meet heavy interest bills and is leaking cash badly. The second phase has been put on hold until the first can pay its way. Most observers accept that the project will eventually need some sort of re-financing, possibly a rights issue.

Under French law, the process of implementing the redundancies could take three months. The company insists that none will take place among staff who deal directly with visitors. The news prompted a 10p rise in the share price on the London market to 620p.

[Martin Waller, Deputy City Editor, *The Times*, 19/10/93]

Read the information given. Answer **all** the questions.

(a) (i)   In the context of the articles, explain what you understand by the following:
- *fixed costs* (article **A**)   (4)
- *rights issue* (article **D**)   (4)

   (ii) Comment on how Euro Disney shares have performed against the F.T. All Share index (article **B**).   (4)

   (iii) Explain the factors which have affected the fall in the price of Euro Disney shares. (15)

   (iv) Evaluate the alternative solutions available to Euro Disney to combat their loss making situation.   (15)

(b) (i)   Explain the concept of the *Product Life Cycle*.   (5)

   (ii) Explain the relevance of this concept to Euro Disney.   (8)

   (iii) Discuss the marketing strategies Euro Disney could employ to extend the life of its theme park.   (15)

(c) (i)   Explain the rationale behind cutting 950 management and administrative staff jobs and not the jobs of those who deal directly with visitors.   (10)

   (ii) As Personnel Officer for Euro Disney, write a draft statement to issue to staff calling for voluntary redundancies.   (10)

   (iii) Identify the factors likely to effect the success of the strategy of voluntary redundancy.   (10)

Oxford and Cambridge

This is a part of Business Studies which you may think is hard because of the use of numbers. However, you generally will only be asked to carry out simple arithmetical calculations. This is not A Level Accounts, so book-keeping skills are not required. It is important to be able to interpret the main accounting statements, not to be able to construct them.

Whatever the size of a firm, it must obtain money and make decisions on how to use it. A **cash flow statement** shows the sources and uses of funds. You must know the different sources of **capital** and the criteria firms would use in deciding where to get funds. A knowledge of the special problems faced by small firms is required. Whether the source is a bank, the stock market or **retained profits**, the firm will have to weigh up the benefits and costs of any **investment**. This is known as **investment appraisal**, and requires knowledge of **payback**, **average rate of return** and **discounted cash-flow techniques** at either **internal rate of return** or **net present value**.

Other accounting statements that you should be able to understand are the **balance sheet**, **profit and loss account**, and **cash flow forecast**. The balance sheet is a snapshot of a business on a particular day. It shows how much money the firm has in particular parts of the business. Anything the firm owns or is owed is known as an **asset**. If it is an asset the firm expects to realise (turn into cash) within a year it is called a **current asset**. If it is an asset such as a machine or a building, bought by the firm for long-term use, it is called a **fixed asset**. The **liabilities** side of the balance sheet deals with money the firm owes. **Current liabilities** have to be paid within 12 months. This would include **bank overdrafts** and **trade creditors**. The profit and loss account is a financial history book. It shows how well a business has performed in the previous year. If a business makes a profit it must decide whether to re-use it in the business (retained profits) or to distribute it. This is shown in the **appropriation account**. The cash-flow forecast is a financial crystal ball. Using it firms predict what money is going to flow into the business, from e.g. sales, and what money is going to flow out, in e.g. paying for wages, raw materials and electricity. It is a well-known fact that many potentially profitable businesses go bankrupt through poor cash-flow planning. You should understand **working capital** and its management.

In order to be able to analyse the success of firms, we compare different firms and look at them over a sensible time period, e.g. five years. The main method used is **ratio analysis**. You will be expected to know and be able to use a variety of ratios, e.g. the **acid test ratio**, the **current ratio**, the **gearing ratio**, and the **return on capital employed**. You must also know the limitations on the use of accounting ratios. In reading a company's **annual report**, you will make use of the **chairman's statement** and **directors' report**.

Firms have to make decisions on the policies they are going to adopt on **inflation accounting**, **stock valuation** and **depreciation**. Dealing with inflation has caused accountants nearly as much difficulty as it has economists. The two main techniques applied are **current cost accounting** and **current purchasing power**. As regards stock valuation, the three principal methods are **FIFO** (first in, first out), **LIFO** (last in, first out) and **AVCO** (average cost). Depreciation can be either by the **straight-line method** or by the **reducing balance method**.

1 Which statements, according to company legislation, must every limited company provide in the annual report? (1)

NICCEA

2 Outline the differences between FIFO and LIFO when accounting for stocks. (2)

NICCEA

3 Explain **two** functions of a budgetary system within an organisation. (2)

NICCEA

4 A machine costs £20,000 to purchase. It has a useful life of 5 years and a residual value at the end of this period of £3,000.

Depreciation figures, using the Reducing Balance Method, are as follows:

Year	Depreciation Provision (£)	Net Book Value (£)
1	6,315	13,685
2	4,321	9,364
3	2,957	6,407
4	2,023	4,384
5	1,384	3,000

(a) Explain the term 'depreciation'. (3)

(b) Suggest **three** factors that influence the useful life of an asset. (3)

(c) Calculate the annual depreciation provision using the Straight Line Method. (3)

(d) Compare the Reducing Balance Method with the Straight Line Method of depreciation. (6)

(e) On a graph, show the annual Net Book Value for each of the following methods of calculating depreciation:
   (i) the Straight Line Method
   (ii) the Reducing Balance Method. (7)

(f) Why is depreciation a provision rather than an expense? (3)

AEB

5 Study the information opposite and then answer the questions.

(a) Calculate trading profit as a percentage of sales. (2)

(b) Why is 'earnings per share' greater than 'dividend per share'? (2)

(c) The information states 'sales, profit and margin up'. From the financial information given, how can one tell that the margin has increased? (2)

(d) Give **three** factors which must be considered before using ratio analysis to analyse company performance. (6)

(e) The information suggests that Cadbury Schweppes has broadened the range of its activities by acquiring other companies. Explain **three** different types of integration available to any company and the possible motives for their use. (6)

AEB

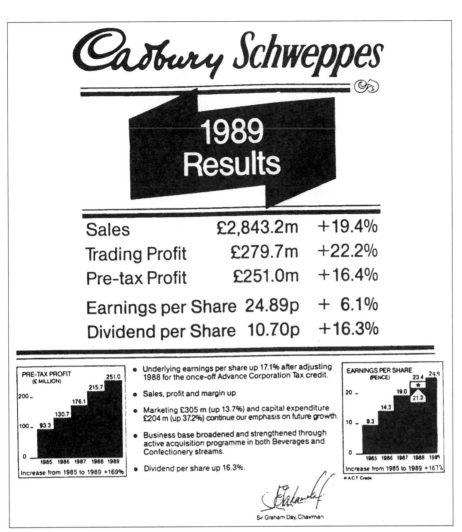

(Source: *Sunday Times*, 4 March 1990)

6 Answer **all** parts of this question.

The wheels of fortune

'I hate to say this Spiro, but it's now June and unless you do something quickly, you'll be out of business in a few months.'

Spiro was surprised at his wife, Maria, making such a harsh statement. He'd come home that evening in triumph. He felt his second-hand car business was really taking off at last. He had just agreed a contract to supply a local car hire firm with 30 cars; ten in September, ten in October and the remainder in the following August. He had also agreed to buy back their used cars. This he felt was a good way of reducing the time and effort spent searching for and buying cars for stock – an activity which had become an increasing burden as his business had grown.

He knew he could obtain the twenty cars for September and October by buying five per month until then, and certainly he felt he could average a 25% mark-up when he sold them, because he would buy them for cash from private owners. Given this guaranteed increase in business, the possibility of setting up a repair and servicing shop looked increasingly likely some time in the future. After all, preparing his existing stock for sale was already taking up more time in the workshop.

His business certainly had grown since it started four years ago. He now had thirty cars on his forecourt, for which on average he had paid £2,300. Experience – and Maria's detailed knowledge of maths – told him he could expect a 30.45% mark-up on them. He did not expect the figures to alter on these non-contract sales, which he thought he might treat as a separate profit centre – a term he had heard Maria use, but which he did not completely understand!

Over the past year he had sold an average of twelve cars per month, and he felt he could sell more if only he had a larger stock from which customers could choose. This was the reason why he had always increased the number of cars for sale by two more per month than he had sold in the previous month. It was a policy he was determined to pursue whatever happened to the contract with the car firm.

Other, more subtle changes had occurred, however. His cars were newer, and consequently more expensive, and although he kept his prices very competitive, he wondered if his garage's location, in a slightly rough part of town, was putting off some customers.

The increase in business had led to the hiring of George, a retired teacher, five mornings per week to help Ron – Spiro's only other employee. Ron had been under a lot of pressure before George's arrival, what with the cleaning and preparation of the cars, and increasingly with the buying and selling of the stock. Spiro dealt with all the paperwork, although in reality that side of the business was dependent increasingly on Maria's expertise. Ron wasn't too good with numbers, although he had an instinct for the price of cars which only Spiro could match. Like Maria, Ron hadn't seemed too enthusiastic about the new contract, but Spiro thought the 10% rise in salary, planned for all the staff from next September, should be enough to keep Ron happy.

Spiro's thoughts were interrupted by Maria speaking. 'We'll have to put together a cash flow forecast,' she said.

Spiro dreaded these moments, when Maria started using words he only half understood. Next she would start asking him for figures he couldn't remember, or quote others at him which were only vaguely familiar.

'At the end of last month you had £20,000 in cash, and your overdraft was £35,000. I believe you have a £50,000 limit on that, haven't you?' Spiro nodded.

'Right, now how much do you think you will have to pay for the twenty contract cars you'll need by October?'

'Well, it's obviously hard to say, but if I pay cash for them and buy five per month from July, I wouldn't want to spend more than £4,000 on average for each of them.'

'OK, we'll work on that, although I'm not too sure about buying them in that way,' Maria said as she started jotting down some figures.

'And when will you be paid for them?'

'In five equal monthly instalments from September.' Maria looked at him sharply, shook her head, and then said,

'OK, now remind me of your normal trade. I know it's seasonal, but if we work on the last twelve month's average we won't be far out.'

Spiro gave Maria all the details, including the following:

Monthly wage bill: £2,500											
Overheads and materials: £000's											
June	July	Aug	Sept	Oct	Nov	Dec	Jan	Feb	Mar	April	May
2.0	3.0	2.0	2.0	3.5	3.5	2.0	3.0	2.0	2.5	2.5	2.5

At that moment Spiro felt the strains of being a one man business were almost not worth the effort.

Now answer the following questions:

(a) Assuming an average month, ignoring wages, overhead and material costs, and rounding all figures to the nearest £1, show that Spiro's car business without the contract generated a cash surplus of £3,800 per month. (3)

(b) Construct a cash flow forecast for each of the next four months starting in June.   (10)

   Make and state any assumptions you think necessary.   (3)

   Was Maria right in her forecast.   (2)

(c) Spiro may need to increase his overdraft limit. If you were his bank manager what factors would you consider in granting or refusing his request?   (12)

(d) Using this case study to support your argument, outline the difficulties of running a sole trader business.   (10)

(e) What advice would you offer Spiro about the way he conducts his business in the future?

   (10)

   AEB

5 *Production*

The production department have to interact with each of the other departments in a firm. If the marketing department think that increased sales are likely, they have to ensure that the production department will be able to raise output. Production will have to talk to the accounts department to see if they can afford to buy extra **stocks** of raw materials. They will have to talk to the personnel department if they have to hire more workers. If the rise in demand is long term, they may have to think about producing on a larger scale (**economies of scale**), which involves **strategic management decisions** such as **location**, and **investment** in new factories, machinery or other firms.

Production managers will be very concerned with the process, costs and quality of production. In terms of process, they will be concerned with **job**, **batch** and **flow production**. Job production is where one-off production takes place. Batch production is where a batch (or group) of a product is subject to part of the production process, e.g. being painted, before the whole batch moves on to another stage of the process. Flow production means lots of products are at different stages of production at the same time. Individual products move continuously from one stage to another, without waiting for the batch to be completed. Both batch and flow are mass-production techniques which make use of economies of scale, **standardisation** and the **division of labour** (**specialisation**).

In terms of cost, they are likely to make use of **absorption costing**, **marginal costing/contribution costing** and **break-even analysis**. Absorption costing involves attempting to allocate (absorb) all of a firm's costs, including **fixed costs** (**overheads**), to **cost centres**. Contribution costing does not attempt to allocate fixed costs. Instead it only allocates to an individual product or other cost centre **variable costs** which can be justifiably allocated. When variable costs are deducted from the price, any surplus is the contribution being made towards paying the fixed costs. This is illustrated in break-even analysis. The firm will break even when **total revenue** equals **total costs**. Total revenue is sales multiplied by price. Total costs are made up of fixed costs, which do not vary with output, and variable costs, which increase as output rises. Given the **average variable costs** figure, it is only necessary to multiply it by output to find **total variable costs**. Total variable costs plus fixed costs is the total cost of a given level of output. If this equals total revenue, the firm is breaking even. An alternative way of calculating break-even output would be to divide the fixed costs by the contribution. If, every time one more of the product is made, the price (the average revenue) is more than the average variable costs, then each product is contributing towards paying the fixed costs. The firm just has to divide the fixed costs by the contribution each unit of output is making, to find out how much it needs to make to break even.

Illustrated algebraically:

Total Revenue (TR) = Price (P) × Output (Q)
$TR = P \times Q$
Total Costs (TC) = Fixed Costs (FC) + Variable Costs (VC)
$TC = FC + VC$
Break-even is when TR = TC.

or:

Average Variable Costs (AVC) = Variable Costs (VC)/Output (Q)
$AVC = VC/Q$
TR = TC for break-even, therefore
$P \times Q = FC + AVC \times Q$, simplifying
$(P - AVC) \times Q = FC$, therefore
$Q = FC/(P - AVC)$ or **Q = FC/unit contribution gives break-even output.**

Illustrated graphically and numerically, if a firm incurs £30,000 of fixed costs, then the fixed cost diagram would look like this:

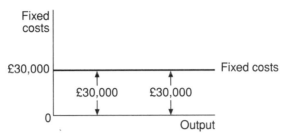

If its average variable costs were £2.00, then the variable cost diagram would look like the diagram below, because VC = AVC × Q. So if Q is 4 then VC is £8, and if Q is 20 then VC is £40.

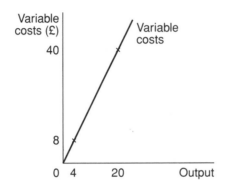

Therefore the total cost line would be parallel to the variable costs, but above it by a vertical distance equal to the fixed cost (i.e. TC = FC + VC, and FC are constant, in this case £30,000; see diagram below).

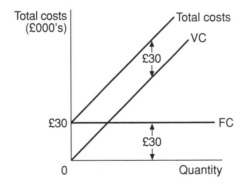

If the price of the product is £5.00, then the total revenue line would look like the diagram below, because TR = P × Q. If Q is 10 then TR is £50, and if Q is 50 then TR is £250.

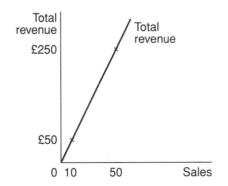

REVISION SUMMARY

If we put total revenue and total cost together, we get a **break-even chart** (see diagram below). Where the two lines cross we know total costs equal total revenue and the firm is breaking even.

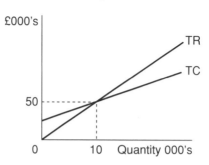

We can confirm that we have drawn the diagram correctly by using either of the methods set out above:

> P = £5.00
> AVC = £2.00
> Contribution is £3.00
> Fixed costs = £30,000
> Fixed costs/unit contribution is £30,000/£3.00
> Break-even output is 10,000.

or: TR = TC

> £5.00 × Q = £30,000 + £2.00 × Q
> If Q is 10,000 then TR is £50,000
> If Q is 10,000 then VC is £20,000; adding £30,000 fixed costs gives us total costs of £50,000, exactly equal to total revenue. So we have got the diagram right: 10,000 is break-even output.

Quality has become a 'buzz word' throughout industry in the last few years. Many firms are introducing **total quality management**. Briefly, this involves a philosophy of **continual improvement** and always **conforming to customer requirements**. Many firms have introduced **quality circles**. These value the ideas of all members of the workforce, not just managers. They give all workers ownership of decisions and responsibility for their work. Workers have been encouraged to see the next person on the production line as their customer who wants **zero defects** in the supplies they are receiving. Many firms have reduced the **levels of hierarchy** in their **organisational structures** and employ fewer people for inspection and supervision. They do not 'inspect in' quality by **quality control** departments, but build it in during the production process. These ideas fit in with the **Human Relations School** referred to in Unit 3, 'People in Organisations'.

If you need to revise this subject more thoroughly, see the relevant topics in the *Letts A level Business Studies Study Guide.*

1   Give **two** examples of the costs that an enterprise may incur in ensuring that its products are
    of a high quality. (2)

    AEB

2   Distinguish between vertical and horizontal expansion. (2)

    AEB

3   Give **three** reasons why a firm would choose to hold stocks of finished goods. (3)

    AEB

4   Give **two** characteristics that may be observed in a firm experiencing diseconomies of scale.
    (2)

    AEB

5   The break-even chart below relates to Arrow soap, a brand of soap made by Smellies plc and
    distributed by Cosgrave Wholesalers to a variety of retail outlets from department stores to
    mini-supermarkets. Sales to retailers are currently 13,000 cases per month.

    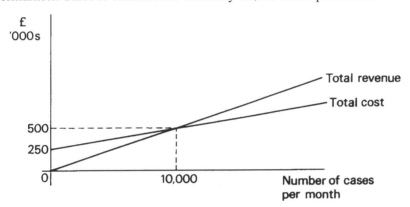

    (a) (i)   Calculate the price per case, the average variable cost per case and the current level
              of profit. (4)

        (ii) What would be the change in the margin of safety if Smellies cut its price to £45?
              (2)

        (iii) Comment on the limitations of break-even charts in decision making. (2)

    (b) Smellies' direct production cost of a bar of Arrow is £0.14. A case of 100 bars is sold
        by Smellies to Cosgrave at £22.50. A bar in a department store retails at £0.59. Define
        'direct production cost' and account for the differences in prices at each stage. (4)

    (c) Explain the advantages and disadvantages to Smellies of using a wholesaler. (5)

    (d) Explain why branding is important to firms like Smellies. (4)

    (e) After a customer complaint, Cosgrave has just checked a delivery of 20 cases of Arrow
        from Smellies by taking a sample of 5 bars. It has found one bar which is discoloured
        and has rung Smellies to say that the whole batch is being returned 'as it is 20%
        defective'. What action would you advise Smellies to take in these circumstances? (4)

        UCLES

6 Read the article and answer the questions which follow.

Prime movers

Stocklin Limited is the wholly owned UK subsidiary of the Swiss materials handling specialist company, Walter Stocklin AG. It is one of a number of European based organisations that has chosen to locate its UK operation at Aston Science Park, Birmingham.

Two years ago, under the direction of Bill Strickland, Stocklin Limited was formed. The company has installed materials handling systems across a wide range of manufacturing, distributive and service industries including numerous companies such as Nationwide Building Society, Walkers Crisps, and Proctor and Gamble.

Stocklin Limited works in close collaboration with another Swiss company which   5
also has its UK headquarters at Aston Science Park. In fact, Bill Strickland reports that the decision to start-up from Aston was largely influenced by the presence of Sprecher + Schuh Automation Limited – specialists in complementary computer control and software for warehouse applications.

'There were also a number of other factors that we considered important to   10
Stocklin', explains Bill Strickland. 'We appreciate the range of facilities offered by Aston – and the big city environment with its tradition of engineering means that we can draw on a specialist engineering labour pool.'

Through its two Divisions, Stocklin Limited covers all aspects of factory and warehousing materials handling – conveyors, cranes, lift trucks, trailers – equipment   15
for moving anything from pallets through fluids to granules in bulk carrying containers.

The company specialised in designing complete warehousing systems. However, all Stocklin equipment will interface with that of other suppliers – and conforms to European and UK standards.   20

Increasingly Stocklin Limited is being commissioned to install systems in banks and building societies, to store property deeds, stocks and share certificates and wills for clients. 'Many such institutions are centralising their deed stores – which can amount to some 6 million items under one roof. Such facilities need to be fully automated – and that means total accuracy. Without that assurance you could end up   25
with complete chaos!' Bill Strickland points out.

(Adapted from *Aston Science Park 'Venture'*, Vol. 2 No. 6 Autumn 1990)

(a) What is meant by the term 'a wholly owned subsidiary'? (2)

(b) Consider **three** reasons why Walter Stocklin AG decided to locate its UK operation at Aston Science Park. (9)

(c) Why is it important to the success of Stocklin Ltd, that its equipment 'conforms to European and UK standards' (line 20)? (7)

(d) Explain **two** advantages and **two** disadvantages to 'companies such as Nationwide Building Society . . .' (lines 3 and 4) of centralising and automating their document stores. (8)

AEB

7 Dalreoch Athletic Football Club has just issued its Balance Sheet for the year to 31 December. It reads as follows.

	£	£
FIXED ASSETS		
Ground, Equipment and other plant		95,000
CURRENT ASSETS		
Stock	85,000	
Debtors	60,00	
Bank	10,000	
	155,000	
CURRENT LIABILITIES		
Trade Creditors	30,000	
Tax Payable	10,000	
Dividend Proposed	4,000	
Bank Overdraft	38,000	
	82,000	
NET CURRENT ASSETS		73,000
TOTAL ASSETS		168,000
CREDITORS		
Term Loans		150,000
NET ASSETS		18,000
Share Capital		12,000
Revenue Reserves		6,000

(a) Analyse the financial situation faced by the club. (5)

(b) Indicate any significant problems the club is likely to face in the short and medium term. (8)

(c) Comment on the 'gearing' of the club. (3)

(d) What recommendations would you make to the club to improve its business position? (4)

(20)
Scottish Examination Board

6 *The external environment*

This is a section of the syllabus that some students find difficult and therefore neglect. This is a major mistake as many examination questions directly question this material and all questions will require an understanding of the external environment. No business operates in a vacuum. They are all influenced by factors beyond their control. Many textbooks refer to these factors as external constraints. These factors include the state of the economy, technological developments, social influences (attitudes, pressure groups, consumer organisations, trade unions and employer associations, etc.), legislation, actions of other firms (competitors, suppliers, purchasers, financial institutions) and European Union and government policy.

If the economy is in **recession**, firms selling goods which are **income-elastic** will find sales falling unless they take appropriate action. They may find themselves under severe pressure from competitors who embark on price-cutting strategies. On the other hand, there may be advantages: the cost of goods from suppliers may be falling and the cost of labour may be cheaper. With a pool of unemployed labour to choose from it may be easier to recruit and retain skilled workers.

If the economy is in the middle of a **boom**, the points made above are reversed. In particular, firms may suffer from the effects of **inflation**. Inflation is best defined as a fall in the value of money. This means any savings (reserves) firms have will buy less and less. Firms will face rising costs for raw materials and may face labour disputes as workers seek to increase their wages to maintain their living standards. If the rate of inflation is higher in the UK than in competitor countries, then UK firms will face tough competition. This competition will occur in both overseas markets and in domestic markets as foreign firms will become more price-competitive in each market. The **balance of payments** will be affected and there may be a fall in the **exchange rate**. A fall in the foreign exchange value of the pound (sterling) will affect different firms to a greater or lesser extent and in a variety of ways. (**NB**: You will be expected to be able to make a distinction between a domestic fall in the value of money and a **depreciation** in the exchange rate.)

Governments are very likely to alter their **economic policy** in response to the economic difficulties outlined above. If inflation is getting out of control, the government is likely to raise **interest rates.** They hope that this will have the effect of reducing consumer borrowing and encouraging saving. Both of these will reduce consumer spending and therefore lower **demand-led inflation**. However, high interest rates also increase the cost of borrowing for firms and therefore discourage them from **investment**. This means UK firms may be technically behind foreign firms when the government allows demand to grow again. It may also sow the seeds of future inflation as the UK firms lack the **capacity** to meet increased demand, not having been able to afford to invest in new plant and machinery. Their response to increased demand may therefore be to raise prices and the inflationary cycle can start all over again.

If you need to revise this subject more thoroughly, see the relevant topics in the *Letts* A level *Business Studies Study Guide.*

Governments can influence firms in all kinds of other ways. They can raise **income tax**, **corporation tax, value-added tax, customs and excise duties**, **national insurance contributions**, etc. They can change the way the welfare state operates. They can **nationalise** or **privatise** industry. They can take a **laissez-faire** attitude to **free markets** or believe in **central planning**. Much more likely is a belief in a **mixed economy**, but the degree of mix varies with different governments and at different times.

Governments also affect firms through **legislation**. We have had legislation covering **consumer protection, monopolies, trades unions** and **labour relations, health and safety** and **the environment**. You will be expected to know the main features of recent legislation and its effects on firms. Since we joined the EEC (now the **EU**) it has become an increasing source of legislation affecting firms. European Union law takes precedence over domestic law and has had a significant impact on, for example, the law covering part-time workers. Membership of the EU has the advantage for UK firms of their being part of the world's largest and richest domestic market. It also means that they are open to very stiff competition without the protection of **tariff barriers**.

Changing **social attitudes** have a big impact on the behaviour of firms. Over the centuries attitudes to women, and to people of different races, colour or religion have changed considerably.

Firms which are thought to be behaving badly may be subject to legislation, or action from workers or consumers. Workers expect to be treated as equals not as menials. Many consumers and investors expect firms to behave **ethically**. **Environmental/green** issues are much more prominent than they were fifty years ago. People will protest in a variety of ways against firms whose actions they disagree with. They may take a firm to court if they think it is breaking the law. They may mount a consumer boycott, e.g. the anti-apartheid movement successfully persuaded many firms to stop trading with South Africa before it called free elections. They may start publicity campaigns which could damage sales or labour recruitment, or reduce sources of finance. They may take illegal action, as have some of the animal rights activists. Some firms have benefited greatly from being linked with environmental issues, e.g. The Body Shop and ethical investment companies.

1 Give **two** factors which have limited the mobility of labour. (2)
AEB

2 How might a fall in the value of the pound sterling affect a firm that imports its raw material and sells its finished product abroad? (4)
AEB

3 Name **three** Acts of Parliament passed for the protection of employees. (3)
AEB

4 Indicate **two** ways in which a high level of unemployment in the economy could affect manufacturing industry. (2)
AEB

5 Below is the text of a leaflet distributed at BP petrol stations in mid-1992.

Side 1

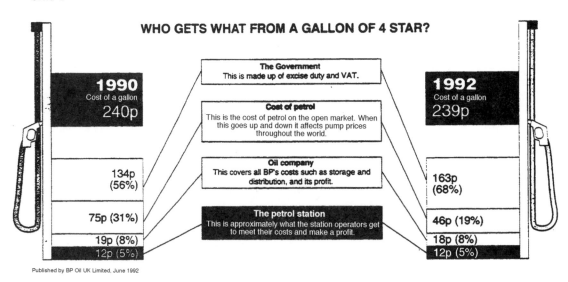

WHO GETS WHAT FROM A GALLON OF 4 STAR?

1990 Cost of a gallon **240p**

1992 Cost of a gallon **239p**

The Government
This is made up of excise duty and VAT.

Cost of petrol
This is the cost of petrol on the open market. When this goes up and down it affects pump prices throughout the world.

Oil company
This covers all BP's costs such as storage and distribution, and its profit.

The petrol station
This is approximately what the station operators get to meet their costs and make a profit.

1990: 134p (56%), 75p (31%), 19p (8%), 12p (5%)

1992: 163p (68%), 46p (19%), 18p (8%), 12p (5%)

Published by BP Oil UK Limited, June 1992

Side 2

PETROL PRICES: THE FACTS

■ **Allowing for tax and inflation, petrol prices are lower now than at any time since 1969.**

The main factor behind pump prices going up and down is the £ sterling value of petrol on the world market. In the main prices keep going higher because of increases in tax, duty and inflation.

Take all this away and today's pump price is about 76p a gallon.

Use the same formula and the gallon price at the height of the Gulf crisis in 1990 was around 113p. Go back five years and it was 83.7p. Ten years ago it was 130p.

■ **Who gets the money you pay for a gallon?**

The lion's share – two thirds – goes to the Government. BP simply collects the money and passes it on. That's fair because it is used to benefit us all. It is not fair however to be accused of profiteering when prices go up because of increased taxation and changes in world market prices. BP gives motorists a fair deal.

That's what the Monopolies and Mergers Commission enquiry concluded in 1990, and BP operates in exactly the same way now as then.

(a) Explain fully the statement 'Allowing for tax and inflation, petrol prices are lower now than at any time since 1969.' (10)

(b) (i) Explain how excise duty and VAT on petrol are levied. (4)

    (ii) Using an appropriate diagram, explain how either excise duty or VAT affect the market for petrol. (6)

(c) Explain the links between

    – the sterling exchange rate and the UK domestic price of petrol

    – the sterling exchange rate and the UK rate of inflation

    – the UK domestic price of petrol and the UK rate of inflation. (15)

(d) Explain **two** economic consequences of a substantial fall in the price of a gallon of petrol in the UK. (15)

UCLES

6   Answer all parts of this question.

David and Maggie's farm

David and Maggie Thomas felt absolutely shattered. Life seemed to have a habit of kicking them in the teeth just as things appeared to be going well. Only four years ago, in 1984, David had been made redundant from the South Wales coal mine in which his family had worked for four generations because, according to British Coal, it was 'uneconomic'. His redundancy money had helped to soften the blow then, but there had been no alternative work for him, other than perhaps going into one of the recently opened Japanese owned factories in the area.

David enjoyed physical work, after all, and he loved the fresh air; probably the result of the years spent mining below the surface. For whatever reason, working inside a factory simply didn't appeal, and as he didn't possess the right qualifications for many other jobs, he decided to look into farming as a second career.

It quickly became clear that this was not an easy option, especially given changes in the European Common Agricultural Policy to reduce agricultural surpluses within the Community. South Wales in particular offered only limited opportunities in farming, and so in 1985 David and Maggie were forced to move to the Bristol area where they bought second-hand an egg-producing unit.

They were thrilled at first, although the costs of buying and keeping the hens appeared astronomical, and continued to rise, until by 1988 the birds cost £200 per hundred to buy and £11.70 per hundred each week to feed, keep warm, and generally look after. The productivity of the hens decreased sharply after one year and so David make it an early policy decision to send his entire flock for slaughter on 31st December each year. Fortunately they had a helpful bank manager who was himself from the Welsh valleys and for a while things looked good.

Nevertheless Maggie never felt entirely welcome in the locality, and she quickly discovered why. The previous owner had exploited the fact that certain farm buildings did not require planning permission from the local authority, and so had constructed his hen houses in what many of the well-off local residents considered to be an inconsiderate position, spoiling the local views. The noise of the feed lorries was also considered intrusive and the chicken waste was both ugly and often smelly. When the original owner had sold out, the locals had hoped that things would improve, and so they were disappointed when David and Maggie bought the farm and re-started production.

David had some sympathy with local feelings but he had a business to run, and it wasn't proving that easy. He was starting up as trends were moving against him. People were eating fewer eggs as they demanded a healthier diet and convenience foods, which meant having fewer cooked breakfasts of bacon and eggs. Nevertheless, David's farm was an efficient unit and he felt he could survive until other, less economic producers, left the market and the price recovered.

Indeed, as 1988 progressed, this did in fact happen, and egg prices rose to 47p per dozen for producers. As a result, on 1st July, David bought 1,000 new birds which doubled his production. Of course this also doubled his running costs but it utilised a second hen house, which until then had been lying idle. Since each bird produced an average of 1.5 eggs per day, both David and his bank manager felt confident that if prices averaged out at 46p per dozen for the year, as seemed likely, the investment would be worthwhile and would help David achieve his personal target of £15,000 per year net profit.

Everything went wrong at the start of December 1988. Following remarks by a junior government health minister, there was serious concern about the contamination of eggs by an organism called salmonella enteridites. This organism can cause illness in all people but can be particularly dangerous to young children, the frail and the elderly. The main reason for the outbreak, it was claimed, was the egg industry's use of cheap, but contaminated, feed for hens, a claim which egg producers strongly denied.

There was a dramatic reduction in egg sales nationally and by 18th December they were half their normal level. The price of 46p per dozen upon which David had based his relative prosperity dropped almost overnight.

Clearly David had to act quickly and so he noted two alternatives which sprang to his mind:

1. Sell some or all of the birds for slaughter. The price offered on 1st December was £180 per hundred.

2. Wait for the government to step in to help out, as rumours suggested it might. If the rumours were correct, unsold eggs would be bought at only 20p per dozen.

Clearly Christmas 1988 was not going to be a season of great joy.

(a) External factors can have a major impact upon small firms. Outline **five** which might have affected David's business. (10)

(b) In 1988 David estimated that his costs would be as follows:

	£
Administration expenses	1,000
Depreciation of capital assets	2,000
Net cost of flock replacement*	200
Loan interest	3,000
TOTAL	6,200

*Assumes 1,000 laying hens costing £200 per hundred, less slaughter revenue of £180 per hundred.

Assuming the crisis of December 1988 had not occurred, demonstrate whether or not David would have achieved his profit objective. Show all your workings. (10)

(c) Following the crisis, what factors should David take into account when considering what he should do next? (10)

(d) There is information in the case to support the view that businesses sometimes put profit before people and the environment. Discuss the reasons why they might modify such behaviour. (10)

AEB

7   Read the article and answer the questions which follow.

Producing a recovery

A number of economic statistics released recently have suggested that recovery is under way. None is more important than the manufacturing output figures. We need to produce, rather than consume, our way out of recession. Figure 1 shows how three key elements to recovery have behaved since recession began in 1990. (Industrial production is made up of manufacturing output plus the production of oil, gas, etc.)   5
Several 'blips' helped to persuade many forecasters to predict recovery in 1992.

What makes 1993 different from 1992?

The short answer is the sharp depreciation of the pound since ERM membership was suspended. The pound's fall has lowered the price of UK manufactured goods by roughly 15% compared with those of their international competition. Furthermore, it   10
has coincided with sharp improvements in productivity and declining wage growth which together are reducing UK manufacturing's unit labour costs and adding to the price advantage.

Between 1985 and 1990, UK manufacturers' share of industrialised countries' exports rose from 7.8% to 8.3%. UK exports grew by 45% while those of all the main   15
manufacturing countries rose by 38%. Price competitiveness is better than in the late 1980s. There is evidence that non-price competitiveness has improved in recent years. If that improvement has been sustained, as we believe, there is good reason to expect that the current level of price competitiveness will result in further gains in market share. Growth in market share will be important for UK manufacturers, since it is   20
likely that the markets themselves will grow only slowly in aggregate in the short-term.

Figure 1

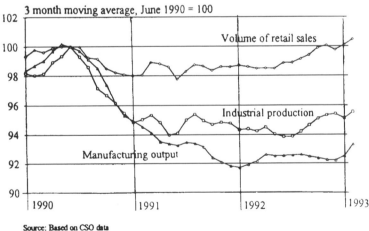

SIGNS OF RECOVERY

Source: Based on CSO data

(Adapted from Lloyds Bank Economic Bulletin, No. 173, May 1993)

(a) (i)   What is the purpose of a 'moving average'?   (1)

(ii) How is a 'three month moving average' calculated?   (3)

(b) From **Figure 1**

(i)   analyse the trends for retail sales and manufacturing output from June 1990;   (6)

(ii) comment upon the signs of continuing recovery shown for industrial production and manufacturing output since the start of 1992.   (3)

(c) Outline **two** dangers for UK business of the recovery being consumer led (line 3).   (4)

(d) Discuss **two** ways in which UK exporters might benefit from the economic factors described in lines 8 to 16.   (4)

AEB

8 Read the following passages carefully and then answer the questions that follow.

A

*Paper cups may be more damaging to the
environment than their polystyrene rivals*

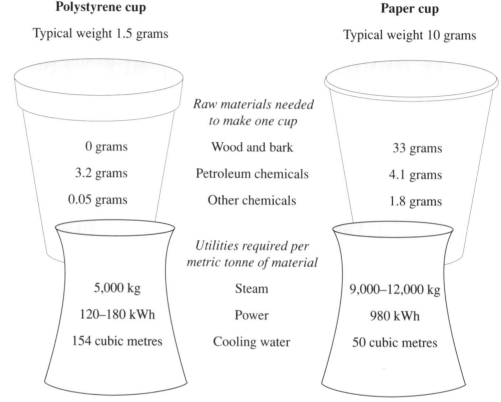

Polystyrene cup		**Paper cup**
Typical weight 1.5 grams		Typical weight 10 grams
	Raw materials needed to make one cup	
0 grams	Wood and bark	33 grams
3.2 grams	Petroleum chemicals	4.1 grams
0.05 grams	Other chemicals	1.8 grams
	Utilities required per metric tonne of material	
5,000 kg	Steam	9,000–12,000 kg
120–180 kWh	Power	980 kWh
154 cubic metres	Cooling water	50 cubic metres

*Paper cup manufacture produces 580 times more waste water
than polystyrene cup manufacture*

The much maligned polystyrene cup, accused of serious crimes against the environment and a byword for the careless modern world, may do significantly less damage than many claim. Compared with the environmentalists' darling, the fêted paper version, the polystyrene cup is a much "greener" container for fast-food drinks, causing less river, land and air pollution.

A spokesman for McDonald's, the fast food chain, said yesterday that the company had always believed that foam cups were more environmentally friendly. She said: "Ironically, we are now having to switch away from polystyrene because our customers believe it is ecologically damaging and we are studying alternative materials."

[From: *The Times*, 14/2/91]

B

Did you know? Nº2

CHLOROFLUOROCARBONS (CFCs) – The Facts

Because McDonald's has always been very conscious of all issues relating to the environment, early last year the decision was taken to cease using CFCs in packaging.

CFC's may be found in refrigerators, aerosol cans, air conditioners, foam furniture and packaging. Other manufacturers have also banned CFCs from their products and it is expected that there will be a sizeable cut in the use of CFCs in the early nineties.

The news from the Antarctic, though not yet conclusive, is deepening international concern. Ozone is perpetually created and destroyed by the sun's radiation from which it, infact, protects us. This sensitive balance is believed to be upset by the release of CFC's through the atmosphere, into the stratosphere.

McDonald's UK packaging supplier was instructed to investigate and implement the best non-CFC alternative. This change-over was completed in April 1988 and all McDonald's foam packaging produced in the UK is now CFC free and carries the CFC FREE message, reassuring customers of this change.

This change in the manufacturing process does not affect the quality of the packaging or McDonald's ability to serve customers with hot, fresh products.

For further information, please write to:
The Public Relations Department
McDonald's Restaurants Limited
11-59 High Road
East Finchley
London N2 8AW

OZONE FRIENDLY

McFACT CARD

McDonald's

THIS INFORMATION IS PRINTED ON RE-CYCLED PAPER.   1/90

[Courtesy of McDonald's Restaurants Limited]

The discussion concerning paper or foam cups has again raised the issue of using crockery at McDonald's, the fast food chain.

(a) Considering both customer reaction and the interests of the firm, what arguments can be put forward for the introduction of crockery? (10)

(b) Both the Personnel and Finance Directors are opposed to the suggestion of using crockery. On what grounds might they argue against its use? (10)

(c) As Managing Director, what decision would you want the Board to make? Explain your view. (6)

Oxford and Cambridge

7 *Decision making*

All organisations are constantly faced with making decisions. Some of these are **strategic** and therefore should be made by the most senior staff, as they have long-term implications for the viability and direction of the firm. Lower-level managers will have to make **tactical** decisions implementing the firm's **mission** (ultimate purpose) in response to current events. Every one of a firm's workers make decisions all the time, though many of these will be habitual. A simple mistake by an apprentice in a chemical plant could lead to an explosion which could have devastating consequences for the locality and the firm. All the various syllabuses ask questions about how firms make decisions and about the techniques which they use. They also expect you to be able to make decisions using the appropriate techniques.

One view is that organisations should make decisions in a systematic manner. The idea is that all decision making should follow the same process. If you study subjects such as Design you will probably have come across it as the design model. In Business Studies it has various names such as the decision making cycle or wheel.

Decision wheel

In the diagram we must start at the centre with how this decision fits in with the aims of the organisation. The next stage begins with collecting evidence to help make the correct decision. Moving clockwise around the wheel alternative solutions are examined. Then the decision is made, planned and implemented. It is then vital to review the decision in order to help future decisions as this is an ongoing cycle which starts again immediately. The diagram below is more sophisticated, putting a specific decision into context. Firms face **internal constraints** such as lack of resources and limitations in the skills and aptitudes of managers and other employees. They also suffer from **external constraints** such as the state of the market and government policy. These constraints are outlined in the earlier units of this book.

If you need to revise this subject more thoroughly, see the relevant topics in the *Letts* A level *Business Studies Study Guide*.

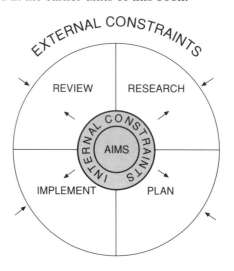

One technique used to decide between alternative courses of action is to draw a **decision tree**. The organisation calculate the probabilities of a particular alternative taking place and the consequent effect on their finances. These are only an aid to decision making as they involve forecasting an uncertain future and calculating odds which are about as reliable as a betting shop's. This should not be confused with **critical path analysis**, despite the fact that the diagrams look similar. In this case, organisations look at a particular project and try to work out the shortest time in which it could be completed. Some activities can be taking place simultaneously, while some cannot start until others are completed. Take the task of making breakfast. It is possible to make a pot of tea at the same time as cooking the toast, but you would not butter the toast until after it was cooked.

George Dowling plc

George Dowling plc is a well-established public joint stock company manufacturing a wide range of paper products. Formed in 1898, it now manufactures at three factories (mills) each of which specialises in a particular product range. These are located in Scotland (paper cartons), North Wales (computer and duplicating papers) and South East England (writing papers). The Head Office is in Birmingham and centrally records all trade enquiries, sales and accounts.

One main market area is that for high quality writing paper for business use. As for other forms of paper manufacture, the basic flow production process involves mixing wood pulp (or in some cases recycled paper pulp) with water to make the paper, which is rolled and wound on to reels. Bulk paper can then be cut and stacked in appropriate sizes before being packaged by wholesalers for various markets. Quality of paper will depend on a number of factors including strength, thickness, texture and colour consistency.

George Dowling plc was in the fortunate position of being the market leader in this quality business paper market and, in spite of the poor economic climate of the past few years, had actually managed to increase its market share in a virtually static market with its brand, Topsheet, which was only made at its factory in South East England. It was, however, experiencing two significant problems with Topsheet, both of which were adversely affecting profitability.

Problem 1

This concerned the quality of production at the factory in the South East, the location of which had originally been chosen to utilise the local water source, now owned by George Dowling plc. The water is extracted from wells and pumped through old Victorian metal pipework to the paper mill. Although the water source is still sound, continuing deterioration of the pipework causes occasional impurities to contaminate the mix, producing discoloration of the final product.

Resulting quality problems have reduced company profit because George Dowling plc now has to sell a proportion of their output as of second quality at reduced prices and recycle badly affected product. On current performance, 80% of output in 1993 was of first quality, half of the remainder was saleable as "seconds" and the rest recycled. (Contributions made by these are given in Appendix A.)

At a recent Board meeting Bob Rollinson, the production director, had outlined four possible approaches to the problem:

Option 1 involved replacing all of the underground pipework with modern plastic pipes. This would cost some £100,000. Once in place, the new pipework would be maintenance-free.

Option 2 was to install a series of filters at appropriate points in the existing system. This was an untried procedure but suppliers were confident that there was an 80% chance of complete success with a 20% chance that the impurity problem would be reduced by half. The cost of installing this option was £40,000 with an annual service cost of £7000.

Option 3 would abandon the wells altogether and buy water from the local water company. This was estimated to cost £30,000 a year, at current prices. George Dowling plc was already subject to regulations imposed by the water company in relation to water extraction and the discharge of effluent (liquid waste) and Bob feared that Option 3 would lead to further constraints on their activities. He was also concerned that water prices would rise faster than the retail price index as they had done in recent years. Publicity associated with such a change might also draw public attention to the social costs involved with the paper-making process.

Option 4 would continue to use the existing pipework.

It was clear that Option 1 would almost certainly solve the impurity problem but further discussion at the meeting had left Bob and the firm's accountant to evaluate the costs and risks involved in all options. Market data is also given in Appendix A.

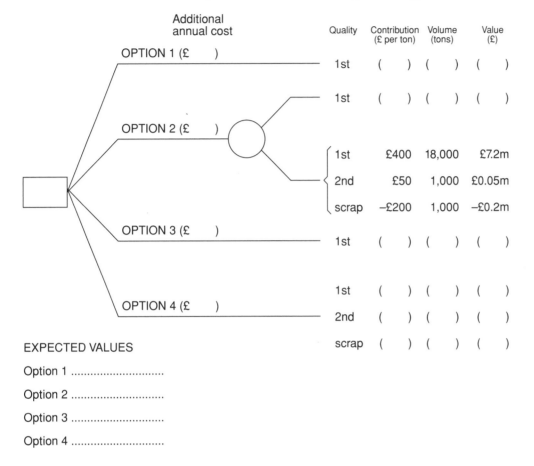

EXPECTED VALUES

Option 1 ....

Option 2 ....

Option 3 ....

Option 4 ....

Appendix A

George Dowling plc average contribution by quality

	£ per ton
Topsheet (1st quality)	400
2nd quality	50
Recycled scrap	−200

UK business paper market sales by volume (tons)

Year	UK total paper	UK total quality paper	Topsheet (G. Dowling)
1993	95,500	43,400	17,600
1994 (forecast)	98,000	44,500	18,000

Appendix B

1993 regional sales of quality paper by volume (tons)

	UK total	Topsheet
London & South East England	21,000	11,200
Midlands & East Anglia	12,200	4,000
Wales & South West England	6,900	1,300
North of England & Scotland	3,300	1,100
TOTAL	43,400	17,600

1 (a) (i) Bob Rollinson calculates the annual cost of Option 1 to be £20,000 and of Option 2 to be £15,000.

Assuming straight line depreciation over a 10-year period in both cases and an annual cost of capital of 10%, demonstrate how you think that Bob arrived at these figures. Has he made any other assumptions? (5)

(ii) Calculate the amount of 2nd quality paper and recycled paper produced if 'Topsheet' is to satisfy its forecast market demand in 1994, assuming no modifications are made to the pipework (Option 4). (5)

(b) (i) Complete the Decision Tree and Table on Insert 1 using your results from Question (a) and other information in the case study. (8)

(ii) Calculate the expected values for each Option, showing your answers in the spaces provided on Insert 1. (4)

(iii) Which Option would you recommend on the basis of your analysis? (1)

(iv) What other factors would you recommend that Bob Rollinson considers before making a final decision? (7)

UCLES

2 (a) Discuss the advantages to Neil and Brian* of using Critical Path Analysis (CPA) in the management of production. (6)

(b) The following inter-related activities make up a typical schedule for one month.

ACTIVITY	DURATION (Days)	DEPENDENCY	COST SLOPE (£ per day)
A	3	–	50
B	3	–	200
C	2	–	150
D	4	A	75
E	5	C	100
F	7	B	200
G	12	D, E	100
H	3	F, G	100
J	6	F	50
K	6	H, J	150
L	10	F	80

(i) Draw a diagram to set out this project as a network. (12)

(ii) Calculate each activity's total float and free float. (8)

(iii) Identify the project's critical activities. (2)

(c) On day 19, Neil and Brian become aware of the fact that activity G will over-run by two days. Any delay in the completion of the project will invoke penalty payments. No single activity can be reduced by more than 1 day.

(i) Determine the minimum expenditure needed to ensure that the project is completed on time, and explain your answer. (6)

(ii) What factors should Neil and Brian take into account in deciding whether to incur this extra expenditure. (8)

(d) In the last year two sub-contractors failed to deliver items on time. The first sub-contractor wrote five articles, one of which was late. In contrast a photographer who supplied photos on 20 occasions was late twice. Both sub-contractors are supplying items for the next issue.

Stating any assumptions you make, calculate the probability that:

(i)   both sub-contractors will be late, (4)

(ii) one of the sub-contractors will be late. (4)

It is not necessary to know about Neil and Brian to answer this question.

UCLES

3 In the Multiproducts Company, consideration is being given to improving profits. The company has two main product lines. Cost and revenue details are given below.

	Product Line 1	*Product Line 2*	*Total*
Average price (£)	20.0	23.0	–
Volume (millions of units)	5.0	4.0	9.0
Total revenue (£m)	100.0	92.0	192.0
Direct materials (£m)	30.0	27.0	57.0
Direct labour (£m)	20.0	13.0	33.0
Direct production costs (£m)	15.0	16.0	31.0
Total direct costs (£m)	65.0	56.0	121.0
Indirect labour (£m)	10.0	12.0	22.0
Depreciation (£m)	10.0	8.0	18.0
Marketing (£m)	3.0	4.0	7.0
Research and development (£m)	1.0	2.0	3.0
Administration (£m)	1.0	1.0	2.0
Total indirect costs (£m)	25.0	27.0	52.0
Net profit (£m)	10.0	9.0	19.0

The main discussions centred upon various strategies:

(i)   changing the price of Product Line 1

(ii) backward integration in Product Line 2, i.e. producing components at present bought in

(iii) contracting out the assembly of products to a firm specialising in this.

The first two strategies were provisionally decided upon and research produced the following information:

(i)   *pricing strategy for Product Line 1:*

A 5% increase in the average price would mean accepting a fall in volume of 10%.

(ii) *backward integration for Product Line 2:*

This would lead to the following changes:
Direct materials would fall by £8m;
Direct labour would increase by £1m;
Direct production cost would increase by £2m;
Depreciation would increase by £1m.

(a) (i)   Calculate the effect on net profit for Product Line 1 of the pricing strategy. (7)

(ii) Calculate the effect on net profit for Product Line 2 of the backward integration strategy. (7)

(b) Why would profits increase as a result of the backward integration? Suggest **two** advantages other than an increase in profits of implementing this strategy. (7)

(c) Explain **two** factors that should be considered if the company were contemplating strategy (iii). (4)

AEB

4 Study the information and answer the questions which follow.

Watcher Ltd. is a small firm that manufactures high quality pillow cases, duvet covers, and fitted sheets. Solely on the basis of the following figures, the Board of Directors has decided to discontinue producing duvet covers and not to replace them with any other product. This will leave production capacity unused, and fixed costs unaltered.

	Pillow cases		Duvet covers		Fitted sheets		Total	
	£	£	£	£	£	£	£	£
INCOME								
Sales income		100,000		120,000		70,000		290,000
DIRECT COSTS								
Direct materials	30,000		40,000		20,000		90,000	
Direct labour	35,000		50,000		25,000		110,000	
OVERHEADS								
Variable overheads	10,000		12,000		7,500		29,500	
Fixed overheads	15,000		21,400		10,700		47,100	
Total costs		90,000		123,400		63,200		276,600
Profit (loss)		**10,000**		**(3,400)**		**6,800**		**13,400**

Show any appropriate calculations.

(a) Explain to the Board the implications of its decision to discontinue the production of duvet covers:

    (i) in the short term; (6)

    (ii) in the long term. (4)

(b) The Directors decide **not** to discontinue duvet cover production. Outline **two** other options that may be available to them. (6)

(c) One of the Directors suggests that there should be a more structured decision making process. What might be the key elements of such a process? (6)

AEB

1 BUSINESS ORGANISATIONS

Candidate's answer	Mark
1 A company with the base of operations in at least two countries.	**2**
2 Equally, i.e. one-third each.	**2**
3 A public corporation is owned by the general public and run by a board appointed by the government, e.g. British Rail.	**3**
4 A public limited company is known as a plc and can sell shares on the stock exchange. A private limited company is known as Ltd and cannot sell shares on the stock exchange.	**2**

Examiner's tip

These answers are brief and to the point. They each gain full marks.

Mark scheme

1 A firm that has production facilities in 2 or more countries. *2 marks*

2 Each partner receives the same amount. *2 marks*

3 Organisations in state ownership but managed by a board appointed by but independent of government. *3 marks*

4 Plc's can sell shares to the general public via the stock exchange.
A private limited company must have Ltd in its name. *2 marks*

---

5 (a) (i) A large established business invests in a smaller often entrepreneurial business in order to collaborate in developing a particular product or market to the benefit of both companies. **4**

Examiner's tip

Though the term may be unfamiliar the answer is contained in the text.

(ii) They prefer it because it is not a permanent arrangement and leaves overall control of the companies unaffected. It is therefore a flexible arrangement. It is probably cheaper, as mergers involve great expense through the use of lawyers, merchant banks, etc. For the small company, they are able to maintain their independence. **4**

Examiner's tip

Four marks are available so four points are made in separate sentences.

(b) (i) The small company may be able to bring new technologies to the large company, as did the companies in the <u>Sunday Times</u>' article. Small companies have many advantages over large companies, in particular they can react more quickly to new ideas. For the large companies, this may be an easier way of entering a new and potentially profitable market. **4**

(ii) The large company often have available finance and greater access to capital markets. They often have greater management expertise. Similarly, they will have well established marketing departments which can be made use of in developing the new products. They have all the benefits of large firms in terms of economies of scale. The small firm can gain by being associated with the established reputation of the large firm. **4**

Examiner's tip

Each of these points is contained in the text. The article is well used.

(c) A culture clash between the different organisations is a potential problem. The two firms may have different missions, e.g. the small firm may want to stay small and may feel their objective is to do good. The large firm may be much more hard-headed and motivated by making profits. The large firm may be frustrated by their lack of control over the small firm. **4**

Mark scheme

5 **(a) (i)** Answers include:
Large business buys or invests in small business. The large business provides business expertise and the smaller new ideas, so both gain.
LEVEL 1
Simple definition. *2 marks*
LEVEL 2
Thorough, developed explanation. *4 marks*

(ii) Answers include:
Independence preserved, cheaper than merger.
LEVEL 1
Identifies 2 points. *2 marks*
LEVEL 2
Explains 2 points *4 marks*

(b) (i) Answers include:
New ideas, responsive, new markets.
Same Levels as (a)(ii).

(ii) Answers include:
Greater funds, management skills, reputation.
Same Levels as (a)(ii).

(c) Answers include:
Different ways of working, different missions, communication difficulties.
Same Levels as (a)(ii).

Maximum 20 marks

6 **(a)** Franchising is where the owner (known as a franchisor) of an idea or business format sells the right to use the idea or format to a franchisee. **4**

(b) **(i)** Annual sales in 1986 £2.2bn, rose to £3.1bn in 1987, i.e. 0.9/2.2 = 40.9%.
Units operated 1986 12,500, rose to 15,000 in 1987, i.e. 2,500/12,500 = 20%.
Jobs in 1986 149,000, rose to 169,000 in 1987, i.e. 20,000/149,000=13.42%. **4**

(ii) The figures suggest that franchising has had substantial success, particularly in the growth of sales. It is also still growing very healthily with the number of units up by over a fifth. The government would be pleased with the impact on unemployment. The franchises also appear to be efficient in that sales grew more rapidly than employment. **5**

(c) **(i)** The advantage to a franchisor of selling the franchise is obviously the revenue gained in selling the franchise itself, which for a McDonalds franchise is substantial. There may also be ongoing royalties and revenue from providing materials. Another advantage is fairly rapid growth of the business. There is also the advantage of letting other people have all the responsibility, risk and work involved in actually running the business. **6**

(ii) The advantage of starting a business to the franchisee would be the purchase of a tried and trusted formula. As the article said, most small businesses fail but a franchise has a very good chance of success. This is because it is less likely to make mistakes and the market is known. There are further advantages in terms of being linked with the reputation of a successful business. This could help in, for example, getting loans. There is also the advantage of having the product marketed on a national basis in a way that a new small firm could never afford. This will help create demand for the product. **6**

Mark scheme

6 **(a)** Answers include:
The franchisor allows an individual or small company (the franchisee) the right to use their business/idea/format in a specific location. The franchisee pays royalties.

LEVEL 1
Simple definition. *2 marks*
LEVEL 2
Thorough explanation. *4 marks*

(b) (i) $0.9/2.2 \times 100 = 40.9\%$ or 41% increase.

$2,500/12,500 \times 100 = 20\%$ increase.

$20,000/149,000 \times 100 = 13.4\%$ or 13% increase.

LEVEL 1

2 calculations correct. *2 marks*

LEVEL 2

All 3 calculations correct. *4 marks*

(ii) Sales per unit are increasing – demand increasing.

Sales per job increasing – productivity increases.

Jobs per unit declining – service or high-tech industries.

LEVEL 1

Describes figures. *3 marks*

LEVEL 2

Explains significance. *5 marks*

(c) (i) Answers include:

Franchisees keen and enthusiastic.

Increased profit at minimum risk.

Growth of business.

LEVEL 1

Simple statements. *1–3 marks*

LEVEL 2

Explains advantages. *4–6 marks*

(ii) Answers include:

Uses expertise of franchisee.

Tried and tested formula.

Track record of success.

LEVEL 1

Simple statements. *1–3 marks*

LEVEL 2

Developed explanations. *4–6 marks*

Maximum 25 marks

---

7 Developing countries are those countries whose living standards have yet to reach those enjoyed by the developed economies, such as those in Western Europe and North America. It is an all-embracing term, but I will take it to mean those countries known as Third World countries, rather than the newly industrialised countries of the Pacific Rim, such as South Korea.

Multinational companies are large powerful companies which have manufacturing bases in more than one country. For example, the Ford Motor Company started in Detroit but now has bases in many countries – the ones I know are the UK, Germany and Spain. This example illustrates that multinationals do not just choose developing countries as their bases.

Developing countries are characterised by great poverty and increasing urban unemployment as people move to the cities. They often have economies which are over-reliant on one or two basic commodities. The problem with being a primary producer is that their prices can fluctuate wildly leading to wide fluctuations in the country's income. These countries will need to export raw materials to the industrialised world in order to be able to import finished products.

We can see from the above description that multinationals will have great appeal. They would have the advantage of enabling the country to broaden their economic base. Being able to produce manufactured goods would reduce their reliance on primary products. It would enable them to reduce the volume of manufactured goods they import. They are likely to be able to export these goods. Any way of improving their often dire balance of payments position is likely to be very welcome. This could have advantages in terms of gaining much needed foreign exchange or even stabilising the exchange rate. Less reliance on primary products may give them the possibility of influencing supply and prices, rather than being subject to the vagaries of market forces. It is certainly easier in response to a recession to reduce the supply of manufactured products than to cut the supply of primary products.

The foreign exchange provided by the multinational when starting (and continuing) its investment will be very welcome. The building of factories, roads, warehouses, etc. is just the kind of infrastructure investment that developing countries need. This is bound to create work for the local economy and demand for local materials. The country will benefit from the cut in unemployment when workers are taken on for the initial building and for the long-term production in the multinational's plant. This fall in unemployment will reduce welfare payments from the government (though these may be small or non-existent). It will also increase the government's revenue in terms of income taxes from the workers and profit taxes on the multinationals. The benefits will be multiplied by the knock-on effects of the increased income on other local firms. An upward multiplier effect should take place, raising income above the initial input from the multiplier.

The multinational will have to train local workers, which hopefully will both widen and deepen the skills base in the developing country. The country will hope that this will help the 'take-off' into becoming a developed country. They will hope that other multinationals will be attracted by the developing skills — broadening them further. In the longer term, they would pray that spin-off locally owned firms would be created by people learning from the business skills of the multinationals.

Sadly there is an opposite point of view. Many people believe that the benefits outlined above do not come to fruition and are outweighed by the drawbacks of the multinationals. Many people are suspicious of the multinational's motives. They feel that the main reason for the multinational transferring bases from the industrialised world to the Third World is to hire cheap labour. This is obviously a disadvantage for workers in the industrialised world, but may also be for the Third World workers. Their desperate need for work may lead to them being exploited. Instead of steadily rising living standards they find wages being held down at poverty levels. The multinationals are very powerful organisations with revenue and profit levels which may dwarf the gross national product of the host country. They may be internationally footloose. They may threaten the host country with withdrawal of their investment unless wages and other costs are not held down. There have been examples in the past of governments having to fit in with the wishes of the multinational companies rather than the other way round. They may demand all kinds of concessions from the host country and put very little back into the local economy. The skilled work may be given to the multinational companies, expatriate workers and the unskilled work to locals. The key research and development work may be carried out in the home country and low level assembly in the host country. These assembly plants may be moved at very little notice.

Examiner's tip

The candidate, as asked for in the question, is now making the case against multinationals. Even if not directly told to it is usually a good idea to produce a balanced argument.

The motivation for siting the plant in the Third World may be to avoid legislation on health and safety, employment rights and environmental protection. The long-term effects on the Third World country on being used as a site for the multinational avoiding these restrictions could be disastrous. The most distressing example of this is the disaster at Bhophal in India where a Union Carbide Plant exploded and the compensation claims have still not been settled.

Examiner's tip

It always impresses an examiner when a candidate uses real world examples. It shows they are not just basing their answers on theory.

To sum up there are benefits and drawbacks when a multinational sets up in a developed country. These will vary according to the ethical stance the multinational takes and the soundness of the Third World country's government. There are good and bad countries and governments. Hopefully the good companies will help a country achieve its development aims. It is another question as to whether that is a good thing!

Examiner's tip

It is always a good idea to sum up. The candidate has produced a well-balanced and well-argued essay. They have referred back to the question to ensure they are answering it. The touch of humour at the end is fine but some candidates overdo this. This would be a Level 5 answer well into the A grade area.

Mark scheme

7   Answers might include:
Benefits to host country: jobs, balance of payments, increased GNP.
Drawbacks to host country: exploitation, damages local industry, damages environment, lack of long-term commitment, political pressure.

LEVEL 1
A knowledge-based answer based on common sense.   *1–5 marks*

LEVEL 2
Either attempts at balanced argument but with superficial analysis or answer showing
element of analysis but one-sided.   *6–10 marks*

LEVEL 3
Well analysed but one-sided or a balanced answer with some analysis.   *11–15 marks*

LEVEL 4
Sound analysis leading towards evaluation.   *16–20 marks*

LEVEL 5
Evaluation of both benefits and drawbacks.   *21–25 marks*

Maximum 25 marks

---

8 **(a)** They fail to see the business as a whole. They over concentrate on the technical side of the business so that marketing, personnel, finance etc. may be overlooked. Many a real business has failed due to concentrating on one aspect.

They lack interpersonal skills which may have led on the one hand to giving Anna Logge too much freedom and on the other hand to being frightened to talk to the managing director of Lockeye Mouldings Ltd. Failure to communicate with Anna led to her resignation. They were not providing Anna with the kind of leadership which would inspire confidence. They were not able to manage their time well. Dealing with Lockeye should have taken priority over the technical demands on their time.

Taking on the Eastminster contract showed their lack of financial acumen. They should have realised the cash flow problems it could cause, and have had the vision to see that the economy could go into recession. Good managers have contingency plans for "worse-case" scenarios. Good decision making looks at all options and weighs up alternatives on the basis of evidence.

In many ways they were laissez-faire managers with all the potential for the anarchy that this can cause.   **10**

Examiner's tip

Uses the case study and links it with more general ideas.

(b) **(i)** Net Profit margin is $\dfrac{\text{Operating profit}}{\text{Total revenue}} \times 100$

Gearing is $\dfrac{\text{Long-term borrowing}}{\text{Capital employed}}$ **2**

(ii) 1985: $\dfrac{96,000}{140,000} = 68.5\%$ 1986: $\dfrac{77,075}{148,500} = 51.9\%$ 1987: $\dfrac{94,752}{171,500} = 55.2\%$ **2**

(iii) The case study says they generated enough profits to keep borrowing down to a minimum. The figures support that so I would expect gearing to be low.   **2**

Examiner's tip

This is clearly set out which helps the examiner. The candidate shows their workings so even if the final answer was wrong, they would get marks if the workings were right. In part (iii) the candidate uses information in the text to confirm that the answer is right.

(c) (i) The business started well. In fact 1985 was their most profitable year. However, they needed premises so profits were bound to suffer in 1986. Taking on Anna Logge may have been a mistake. The business had been growing steadily without her. Her attractive salary package was possibly a cost that would not be paid for by extra orders. The crucial mistake was becoming obsessed with the Eastminster contract at the expense of their other customers. With an expanding staff, they moved to prestigious premises in 1989. Thus by 1991 they were committed to lots of expense when revenue began to suffer in the recession. It is just this combination, often a result of overtrading, which leads to business failure. **10**

Examiner's tip

Has identified points and importantly has explained their significance.

(ii) The critical points were crucial. The high rent payments significantly increased their costs, and taking on new staff, particularly Anna, again put up their costs. The dominance of the Eastminster contract blinded them to other developments and led them to putting "all their eggs in one basket". This led to a loss of contracts and a failure of other contracts to materialise. Either revenue falling or costs rising would be bad enough on their own. The disastrous combination led to the £94,625 loss in 1991. **7**

Examiner's tip

Nice use of both text and appendices. The candidate shows the links to cost and revenues. A good strong finish.

(iii) The critical points largely explain Systech's position. Though linked to their poor decision making, Systech's failure to keep customers happy has led to a fall in revenue. They expected sales to local government which illustrates a failure to research that market well. These matters were to an extent within their control. They were affected by external constraints such as the recession but, as I said earlier, they should have traded cautiously in case of such a fall in demand. Other external influences such as uncertainty over local government finances affected them. They had also been affected by competitors. They had identified a gap in the market. Other firms had seen that Systech were doing well and wanted a share of the action. **7**

(d) Lack of business skills is a common difficulty. Oliver and/or Mike should have taken a business course such as A Level Business Studies. Another common difficulty is concentrating on the product. They should have forced themselves to develop strategic plans. They could have achieved this by using private consultants or government agencies such as their local Training and Enterprise Council. To avoid the dangers of overtrading, the production of cash flow forecasts is an invaluable aid. They would then have recognised the dangers of their rising costs. They could have used other business techniques such as decision trees to work out the likely success of alternative decisions they could make. **10**

Mark scheme

8 **(a)** Answers may include:

Strengths	*Weaknesses*
Computer expertise	Lack of interpersonal skills
Work as a team	Lack of management knowledge
Hardworking	Inability to take tough decisions
Experience	

Candidates may point out other strengths/weaknesses.

LEVEL 1
Brief relevant points listing a number of strengths or weaknesses. *1–3 marks*

LEVEL 2
Fuller analysis/development of points using case theory. *4–7 marks*

LEVEL 3
Evaluation of strengths or weaknesses using case **and** theory. *8–10 marks*

(b) (i) 1 mark for each correct ratio.

(ii) 1 mark for correct method.
2 marks for correct calculations.

(iii) Gearing ratio is low. *1 mark*
Making good profits therefore uses retained profits. *1 mark*

(c) (i) Answers might include:
1. Downturn in the economy.
2. Changes of premises.
3. Employment of marketing specialist.
4. Development of systems package for Eastminster.
5. Failure to satisfy Lockeye Mouldings.

LEVEL 1
Relevant points made superficially. *1–3 marks*

LEVEL 2
Explanation of relevant points. *4–6 marks*

LEVEL 3
Evaluation of critical points in Systech's development. *7–10 marks*

(ii) LEVEL 1
Limited explanation. *1–2 marks*

LEVEL 2
Fuller development/analysis. *3–5 marks*

LEVEL 3
Evaluates importance of different critical points. *6–7 marks*

(iii) Answers might include:
– The recession
– Growing too fast
– Over-reliance on one contract
– Impact of Community Charge

LEVEL 1
Brief relevant points. *1–3 marks*

LEVEL 2
Fuller development leading to evaluation. *4–7 marks*

(d) Answers might include:
- – Management training
- – Balanced management teams
- – Cautious increase in sales
- – Using cash flow forecast

LEVEL 1
Brief ideas but not relating to Systech. *1–3 marks*
LEVEL 2
Explained ideas in relation to Systech. *4–7 marks*
LEVEL 3
Evaluation of possible solutions. *8–10 marks*

Maximum 50 marks

2 MARKETING

Candidate's answer	Mark

1 **(a)** In the market-oriented firm the marketing department is likely to be more influential and may have a larger marketing budget. It will start by identifying customer needs through market research. It will then produce the product people want if it is to be profitable. The product-oriented firm will start with the product it is producing and will try to persuade consumers to buy it through advertising and other marketing techniques. However, if customers do not like the product this will not be successful.

   (b) One FE college with which I am familiar has recently massively increased its marketing using bus and poster advertising and even short films at the cinema. If the marketing department is successful in recruiting students then revenue will be generated. This revenue, like all money in the college, will have to be accounted for by the accounts department. The marketing department will require money for its marketing campaign. The budgets will be provided by and checked by the accounts department.   **8**

Examiner's tip

Brief answers because each section is worth only 4 marks.

2 **(a)** How the demand for a product reacts to a change in price is known as price elasticity of demand. Responsiveness will vary according to whether the product is bought regularly, the proportion of income spent on the product and whether it is addictive. The price of another item will be an influence if that item is either a substitute or a complement for the main product.

   (b) VAT stands for value added tax. The government imposes this tax as a percentage of the price of a product. It would be paid by the book supplier and therefore affects the price at which they would be willing to supply books, as shown in the diagram below. It raises the price of books and is likely to reduce the demand for them.   **8**

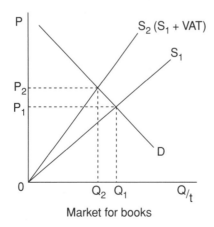

Market for books

Examiner's tip

In this Examiner's opinion it is nearly always a good idea to use diagrams when answering questions involving demand and supply.

Mark scheme

1 **(a)** Distinguishes between market- and product-oriented. Gives an example of different operations.   *2 × 2 points (one for mention, one for development)*

    (b) Any relevant points.   *1 mark for statement plus 1 mark for development 2 × 2*

2 **(a)** Influences on PED – substitutes/percentage of income/luxury/necessity/frequency of purchase.
      Influences on cross-elasticity – substitutes/complements.   *4 × 1*

    (b) Clear explanation and diagram.   *2 × 2*

---

3 **(a)** 10,400/52,000 × 100 = 20%.   **2**

    (b) The demand for the Mini exceeds supply so therefore they are able to keep its price high. When more people wish to buy the car then there are cars available, firms ration them by raising prices. It is in demand because it has achieved cult status in Japan and is regarded as chic in France. This means demand is inelastic; people put up with price rises in order to show off their fashionable cars.   **6**

> **Examiner's tip**
>
> Good use is made of the information provided in the article.

    (c) One product extension strategy that was used was the link with the name Mini Cooper. This associated the product with the successful rally car. The association was not in name only but also in developing the performance and quality of the car. There was also an appeal to environmentalists by cleaning up the car's exhaust gases. The style and look for the car was improved by 'special paint jobs'. Another extension strategy was to develop export markets such as France and Japan. In summary an exclusive niche market was developed where high prices could be charged.   **8**

    (d) The Government could impose taxes (tariffs) on imported cars or impose a quota (limit on the number) allowed into the country.   **4**

    (e) Graham Day must have been convinced in 1986 that the revenue the Mini was worthwhile or that it was going to be profitable in the future. Another alternative is that it was worth keeping in the short term because revenue exceeded variable costs and therefore a contribution was being made to Rover's fixed costs.   **5**

> **Examiner's tip**
>
> A good application of a business concept to an unfamiliar situation.

Mark scheme

3 **(a)** 10,400/52,000 × 100 = 20% or 10,400 : 52,000 = 1 : 5   *2 marks*

    (b) Answers include:
      Demand exceeds supply, elasticity, customer attitudes.
      LEVEL 1
      Identifies points.   *1–3 marks*

LEVEL 2
Explains points   *4–6 marks*

(c) Answers include:
Improved design, better quality, environmental appeal, better marketing, pricing strategy, niche marketing.
LEVEL 1
Brief relevant points.   *1–2 marks*
LEVEL 2
Explains strategies.   *3–5 marks*
LEVEL 3
Evaluates strategies.   *6–8 marks*

(d) Answers include:
Tariffs, quotas, bureaucratic methods, subsidies, health and safety rules.
LEVEL 1
Identifies 2 methods.   *2 marks*
LEVEL 2
Explains 2 methods.   *4 marks*

(e) Answers include:
Revenue, profits, covering variable costs.
LEVEL 1
Identifies justifications.   *1–2 marks*
LEVEL 2
Explains reasons.   *3–5 marks*

                                                           Maximum 25 marks

---

4   The statement in the question is far too simplistic. Customers' decisions to buy a product are based on a wide and complex range of different factors. Furthermore, different customers will react in a variety of ways to a firm's product or service. On top of this the type of firm and the economic, political and social circumstances it finds itself in will influence how well it can sell goods. In the main body of this essay I will analyse these factors and evaluate their influence compared with price.

Examiner's tip

This is an excellent introduction. It shows the Examiner that the candidate understands that the question involves comparing other influences with price. It also shows that the candidate knows evaluation is a key word in the question. Many candidates ignore the title of the question and instead of answering it directly just write all they know about marketing without applying it in context.

The wider context is important. If an economy is deep in a recession, a product that was selling well because consumers thought it was reasonably priced may find itself in difficulty. Lots of examples exist, but we only have to recall how well the housing and car markets were doing in the mid-1980s and how badly they crashed in the late-1980s. Even in 1994, houses that were thousands of pounds cheaper than in say 1988 were not selling. The lower prices were not enough to overcome lack of consumer confidence.

In a similar vein, changes in fashion or social attitudes may affect sales. The Body Shop has made great play of the ethical stance it takes in purchasing and producing products. Consumers who care about these things have been willing to pay higher prices for these Body Shop products than at other high-street shops. The Body Shop as a result has grown rapidly even through the recession. As other retailers have seen this success and have noticed the change in society's attitudes, they have begun to produce similar ranges of products.

This leads neatly on to the effects of competition. Any successful firm, particularly innovative firms, can expect that they will eventually go through periods of competitive turbulence. This is illustrated below on a Product Life Cycle diagram.

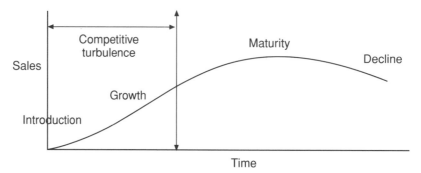

This competition may be so tough that the firm has to abandon selling the product however low its prices.

There are many decisions within the control of firms. Central to these are the so-called 4P's: price, product, promotion and place. The firm must adopt a coherent strategy placing the correct emphasis on these factors appropriate to its product.

As an illustration, let us look at the company/product Filofax. When Filofax was first developed it was seen as an innovative good which would appeal to yuppies (young, upwardly mobile professionals). Products which have a snob appeal must be designed to satisfy that appeal. Hence the product had to be of high quality, e.g. many were bound in leather. The price was high, which enabled the consumer to engage in conspicuous consumption, i.e. showing off wealth through spending on expensive goods. The product was available in high-class shops (as another example, recently certain perfume manufacturers tried to stop their products being sold in shops which they thought would damage their exclusive image). Filofax advertised in magazines which were read by the people in the particular social classification aimed at.

Filofax were initially very successful. In evaluating this success it would be very difficult to assess which of the 4P's was most important. Had they just charged a high price but sold a poor quality product in any retail outlet it is doubtful in my opinion that the product would have been a success.

Examiner's tip

Again marks are being scored here by referring back to the question. Many other candidates would have just listed the 4P's and not have compared them with price. This is good evaluation which moves the marks to the higher levels of the mark scheme.

We do know that subsequently retail outlets such as W H Smith, Woolworth's, ASDA, etc. brought out their own copy-cat brands. This meant severe price competition and also the loss of social cachet in being the owner of a product now available to most consumers. The loss of sales might have been due to the product just being a 'nine-day wonder' like many fashionable products. Or was it that many people decided that the old-fashioned diary was just as useful in meeting their needs? Alternatively, the product may have been affected by technological developments such as the electronic organiser. Whatever the cause, the firm could not rely on price being the sole important factor.

It is certainly the case that different firms, producing different goods at different stages of the product life cycle place entirely different emphasis on the marketing mix. Kwik-Save and Marks and Spencer, for example, both place a lot of emphasis on value for money. But Kwik-Save charge low prices, saying that their no-frills products are good value, whereas Marks and Spencer charge relatively high prices, which they say is justified by the quality of their products. Both firms very successfully appeal to their particular customers. This relationship between price and quality has an important psychological impact on consumers. It is also interesting to note that Kwik-Save advertise extensively on television and Marks and Spencer do not.

To summarise, we can see that firms and consumers will differ markedly in their response to the quotation. A low-priced, high-quality toy that no-one knew about might be thought to be doomed to failure by an advertising executive until it was linked to a children's television series and heavily advertised, creating a distinct brand identity. On the other hand, a production manager might scorn a massive advertising campaign for a poor-quality product, arguing that 'you cannot sell a bad product twice'. A salesperson may believe it is their charm and excellent after-sales service which leads to sales, as opposed to the price of the product. An overseas agent may feel it is their knowledge of the export market and changing attitudes to their home country, rather than price, which is important.

Examiner's tip

It is very useful to summarise and emphasise points. But there are two things to avoid: repetition and making too many points in one sentence. The first cannot gain marks and the second may lead to marks being missed by the Examiner not spotting all the points

---

In my view the importance of price will vary from product to product and also must not be treated in isolation to the other elements of the marketing mix.

25

Mark scheme

4 Likely content:

> Place/distribution.
> Promotion/advertising.
> Market research.
> Quality.
> Delivery times/reliability.
> After-sales service.
> Type of good.
> Market conditions.
> State of the economy.
> Knowledge/desires of purchasers, etc.

Valid examples will be credited throughout.

LEVEL 1
Identified one or more other factor(s) important to selling. *1–4 marks*

LEVEL 2
Offered a simplistic analysis of one or more other factor(s). *5–8 marks*

Repetition of notes cannot gain more than 8 marks.

LEVEL 3
Offered analysis of one or more other factors which are related back to the question **or** offered a simple notion of evaluation, i.e. comparing price with one or more of the alternatives but without making a strong case. *9–16 marks*

LEVEL 4
As Level 3 but making a strong case without an examination of the wider context.

17–21 marks

LEVEL 5
Offered explanations displaying skills of evaluation and perception, perhaps bringing in wider implications such as overseas markets, etc. *22–25 marks*

Maximum 25 marks

---

5 (a) If the market has developed then grocery outlets will very quickly want to share the profits which are being made. Many customers, once they are aware of the benefits of the product, will buy the grocers' own-label product because it is cheaper. If these customers did not exist it would not be worth the grocers producing their own label. Hence profits are a major consideration. The other major influence will be patents and trademarks. If the initial producer has patented the product this will restrict or even stop the development of own labels. **5**

   (b) Advertising elasticity of demand is measured by the formula:

   % change in demand / % change in advertising expenditure.

The market grew by 45m in 1987, from 105m.
45/105 × 100/1 = 42.86%.
Advertising spending increased by 0.5m from 2.0m.
0.5/2.0m × 100/1 = 25%.
AED = 42.86/25 = 1.71.

Any figure above 1 shows that there is a greater percentage increase in demand than the percentage increase in advertising. The firm would obviously be very pleased with this result as revenue will be increasing substantially. **5**

Examiner's tip

It is a good idea to write the formula as this may gain marks even if the calculations are wrong.

(c) The marketing could have been targeted geographically to those places with more 'image conscious trendies', as the company did in targeting London.
   They could target the reading matter of these people in, for example, trendy colour supplements or expensive, exclusive magazines.
   They could have tried to 'place' the product in the restaurants, wine bars, and shops which this target group use, e.g Covent Garden, gourmet restaurants, wine bars, and shops such as Harrods.
   They may have priced the product in such a way that those seeking status thought that only they could afford it **4**

(d) Certainly the strategies outlined above would restrict the market. Prices would have to fall to come within the income and psychological price range of the broader population. Mass markets require mass production, so prices could fall due to economies of scale. It would be vital to sell in supermarkets and pubs in order to get the demand required. Mass advertising would require advertising on TV and in popular newspapers in a style which has a broader appeal. **3**

Examiner's tip

Only 3 marks are allocated to this question so the candidate wisely does not write too much.

(e) People are becoming more environmentally conscious. They are concerned with the amount of pollution which gets into our rivers and reservoirs. They are also more health conscious. They want to drink products which are pure, as opposed to water which may contain harmful minerals. The article also refers to a national water strike in 1983 which doubled the sales. **3**

Mark scheme

5 (a) Answers include raising revenues and profits.

LEVEL 1
Identifies factors. *1–2 marks*

LEVEL 2
Explains factors. *3–5 marks*

(b) Advertising elasticity of demand $= \dfrac{\text{\% change in demand}}{\text{\% change in ad. spend}}$ or $\dfrac{\text{propn change in demand}}{\text{propn change in ad. spend}}$

$$= \frac{42.9\% \ (43\%)}{25\%} \qquad = \frac{45/105}{0.5/2.0}$$

$$= 1.716 \ (1.7). \qquad\qquad = \frac{90}{52.5}$$

$$= 1.714 \ (1.7).$$

LEVEL 1
Correct calculations. *1–3 marks*

LEVEL 2
Calculations and explanation. *4–5 marks*

(c) Answers include: geography, outlets advertising, elitism.

LEVEL 1
Identifies points. *1–2 marks*

LEVEL 2
Explains points. *3–4 marks*

(d) Increase range of outlets, change advertising, change image. *3 marks*

(e) Worries over drinking water, environmental awareness, health consciousness. *3 marks*

Maximum 20 marks

3 PEOPLE IN ORGANISATIONS

Candidate's answer	Mark

1 (a) Having completed my work experience with a small engineering firm I discovered that the Managing Director's preferred recruitment method was 'head hunting'. He had worked for a large company where a number of people had been made redundant. Because he knew these people well and knew that they were good at their jobs he was keen to hire them. Though this seemed to work for him, I would have thought a more systematic method should have been used. There should have been meetings of the directors to decide if extra manpower was required. Then job descriptions and person specifications should have been drawn up. This would enable the firm to have proper criteria on which to judge applicants. Through advertising in a national paper a wider field than just people the Managing Director knew would have been available. Having said this, the only person who I identified as not fitting into this small firm was the only one recruited in the manner most firms use.

(d) In the same firm the Managing Director was excellent at motivating his staff. He had real charisma. He led from the front and worked extremely hard. He had managed to turn round a failing company. This success, I believe, was a major motivator and wanting to work for him inspired the staff. He knew each member of staff personally and always had a kind and encouraging word for them. Obviously this will be more difficult in a larger firm but individual managers could be encouraged to adopt this approach. Involvement of workers in such things as quality circles in a way creates the atmosphere of ownership and responsibility found in small firms.

(e) As you can see from the above, communication was fairly good in the small firm. However, there were potential barriers. The directors were fairly well educated and they may have had problems using the right level of language with the shop floor workers. The directors' offices were only a short distance from the shop floor but at least one of them never left his office, making communication very difficult. The Managing Director was regularly away from the firm trying to drum up business. At these times the business noticeably flagged, according to a firm of management consultants which had reviewed their operations. **15**

Examiner's tip

The candidate has followed the rubric and only answered three parts of the question. They have drawn on their experience, but rather than just describing it they have applied their knowledge of business theory to it. Showing critical understanding of their work experience helped answer the question.

Mark scheme

1 LEVEL 1
Descriptive but relevant answer. *1–2 marks*

LEVEL 2
Hints at critical understanding but limited weak research. *3–4 marks*

LEVEL 3
Thorough research with good critical understanding. *5 marks*

Maximum 15 marks

---

2 (a) There have been many changes in social attitudes to women working. It has become much more socially acceptable for married women in particular to work and hence the significant increase. Over this period there has been a significant decline in manufacturing employment, which in the past has been associated with male jobs. At the same time there has been an increase in employment in the service sector, which has been associated with supposedly female jobs. A further influence has been the pressure to participate in rising living standards by having, if possible, two incomes coming into a family.

(b) There are several explanations, but the most obvious one is that discrimination against women is rife despite the law. Other explanations include women taking career breaks to have a family. This tends to happen just at the point they are building a career, and when they return they find they have gone back to the bottom of the pile rather than to where they were when they left. It may also be the case that women are socialised into not pursuing a career aggressively in the way that some men do.

(c) Again socialisation may play a part. Women may feel that unions are for men and some male trade unionists may knowingly or unknowingly encourage this. The unions may be at fault in not taking the needs of women into account, e.g. by holding meetings at times that are inconvenient to women. Unions tended in the past to be stronger in male-dominated occupations, though this pattern is changing.

(d) Again straightforward discrimination plays a part. The career breaks referred to earlier may stop women gaining promotion. Women are over-represented in part-time work and in sectors dominated by low-paid jobs. The fact that women are under-represented in trade unions may also mean that they miss out on any successes trade unions may have. **16**

> **Examiner's tip**
>
> Sensible use of information in one question to help answer another.

Mark scheme

2 (a) Change in social attitudes/decline in manufacturing, growth in service sector/improved household appliances. *4 marks*

(b) Discrimination/career breaks/social attitudes.
2 points × 2 marks: one for mention, one for development

(c) Male-dominated unions/attitude of unions/non-union sectors. *2 × 2 marks*

(d) Part-time work/over-representation in low-paid work/low unionisation/lack of promotion/discrimination. *2 × 2 marks*

Maximum 16 marks

3 (a) 25th June 1988

To: The Managing Director,
From: The Training Manager.

Quality Circles

Terms of Reference

I have been asked to research and outline four possible benefits to the company of introducing Quality Circles.

Procedure

I researched the literature and visited several companies who use Quality Circles.

Findings

1. Staff become more involved in the work of the firm. There is a greater sense of ownership of decisions in the firm.

2. They have great success in solving job-related problems rather than waiting for supervisors. This obviously saves time and therefore money for the firm.

3. Because people are working in groups they learn to work together effectively and hence team-building is improved.

4. In these groups workers learn from each other and are provided with training to solve problems systematically.

Recommendations

We should implement Quality Circles in our Hampshire factory on a trial basis.

Signed

Fred Flint.

10

Examiner's tip

The correct report format has been used which gains 2 marks. Four advantages have been given as requested. Each point has been explained to gain the development marks.

(b) 1. Quality Circles may be very expensive to establish. People will have to be sent on training courses. The time spent in meetings is at the expense of time spent on production.

2. There may be resentment from the workers who feel that they are being asked to do the managers' work. They may not trust the managers' motives.

3. Managers may think that this is just another trendy idea from the Training Manager. They may feel that it is a waste of time.

4. If the managers think an autocratic style of management is more appropriate then they will question the philosophy behind Quality Circles.

5. Workers may press for wage increases as they are being asked to take more responsibility for their own work.

10

(c) Theory Y takes a very positive attitude to human nature. It assumes that if workers are given responsibility for their work they will welcome it. They will gain greater job satisfaction by being able to make decisions. Quality Circles are a method of putting this theory into practice and hence fit in very well with the theory.   5

Mark scheme

3 (a) Report format – to/from/date/title/terms of reference/procedures/recommendations/ conclusions/findings/headings/signature.   *2 marks*

Answers include: motivation, cost savings, better ideas, improved production.

LEVEL 1
Identifies benefits.   *1–4 marks*

LEVEL 2
Explains benefits.   *5–8 marks*

(b) Answers include: management resistance, worker suspicion, costs, training etc.

LEVEL 1
Identifies problems.   *1–5 marks*

LEVEL 2
Explains problems.   *6–10 marks*

(c) Answers include: increased involvement, taking on responsibility, enjoyment of work.

LEVEL 1
Superficial knowledge of Theory Y.   *1–2 marks*

LEVEL 2
Relates Theory Y to Quality Circles.   *3–5 marks*

Maximum 25 marks

4 (a) Notice boards.
Team briefings.   2

Examiner's tip

Simple answers gain the 2 marks and save time for later questions.

(b) It is very easy to just walk past a notice board and therefore have no idea it has important information on it.

The language on the notice board may not be clear enough for the receivers to understand and they may not have the opportunity to ask for clarification.

The notice board may be so cluttered and irregularly updated that people miss important information.

Meetings are up to date, people can be consulted and feedback can be given immediately.   6

Examiner's tip

The candidate has worked out that there are 2 marks for each point and so has developed each point. If you are uncertain that you have gained all the marks, add another point when you have time.

(c) (i) Staff like to know what is happening in a company. If they feel well informed their morale will be raised.

(ii) In team briefings it is possible to build up team spirit so that people feel part of the organisation.

(iii) One-to-one meetings lead subordinates to feel that their manager values them. They are giving up time for them and seeking their ideas.　　　**6**

(d) One reason is inertia. Once a method has become routine people continue to use it without thinking about its effectiveness. People are naturally conservative about change. A second reason could be cheapness. In the examples, the short suggestion schemes and notice boards are much less expensive in terms of costly management time compared to briefings and meetings.　　　**6**

Mark scheme

4 (a) Team briefings (1) and notice boards (1).　　　*2 marks*

(b) Relies on written word/no compulsion to read/no feedback/one way/no check of understanding/gets out of date so disrupted/no interaction/one at a time/selective reading/boring.

Compared with team briefings/one-to-one meetings. Planned/live/up-to-date/relevant/immediate feedback/listened to/consulted/influence/plus non-verbals.

3 × 1 + 1 for development = 6 marks

(c) Communication and understanding/understanding and confidence/accuracy/feel-good factor/security need/express views/be consulted.

Award correct and relevant relationship with morale;
and/or reference to Maslow, Herzberg, etc.
3 × (1) + (1) mark = 6 marks

(d) Reasons may include:
Cost and time of implementing effective communication methods.
Ignorance of ineffectiveness of communication methods.
Managers' reluctance to change from known format.
May have (perceived) positive effect on motivation.
Internal structure may make effective communication difficult.

6 – up to 3 marks for each reason examined
Maximum 20 marks

---

5 (a) (i) Fixed costs are those costs which do not vary with output. They are costs which will have to be paid even if no customers visit Euro Disney. Such costs would include the rent on the land or interest payments on loans.　　　**4**

A rights issue means selling shares to existing shareholders at a price which encourages them to buy. Euro Disney were considering it because they were suffering cash flow problems. They therefore hoped current shareholders would put more money into the business to safeguard their investment and possibly gain future returns.　　　**4**

Examiner's tip

These are good definitions, well explained and put into the context of Euro Disney as requested by the question. They are also fairly brief as only 4 marks are allocated to each sub-section.

(ii) Two points stand out. Firstly that generally the share price has out performed the F.T. All Share index. Secondly, the trend in its price has mostly mirrored movements in the index. One of the few times Euro Disney fell more rapidly than the index and failed to rise when the index was rising was in the late summer of 1992.

4

(iii) From the answer to (ii) it can be seen that Euro Disney shares fall when the All Share index is falling. All shares will be affected by sentiment in the City and by the state of the economy. In the former case speculation that share prices will fall will lead to people selling shares. Once more people wish to sell shares than wish to buy, the fall in price becomes a self-fulfilling prophecy. The latter is affected by real factors such as falling demand for goods and services, falling output and rising unemployment. A recession may lead to business profits falling and therefore shareholders may wish to sell their shares.

There are also factors which are specific to Euro Disney as set out in Article B. The firm put out a statement saying it was not going to make a profit even in the summer months. This could mean no dividend to shareholders. The reason the firm was not making a profit was that the recession had badly hit the French tourist industry. There were therefore fewer visitors to the theme park. In addition, those who did visit were spending less than expected on merchandising both in the park and in the hotels. This lower revenue would make it difficult to cover costs. Visitors were also discouraged by the weather, the surly staff and high prices, and were attracted instead to Paris. The tourist industry had also been hit by a fall in the value of sterling, the lira and the peseta. This made it more expensive for foreigners to visit France. To illustrate this, if the price of a ticket to Euro Disney was 100 francs, the cost to a British visitor when the exchange rate is F10 : £1 is £10. If the pound loses value so £1 can only buy 4 francs (F4 : £1) then the cost of a ticket rises to £25. It is easy to see that this will put off visitors, particularly families.

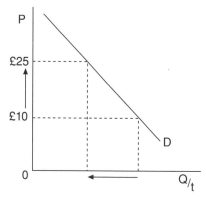

The demand curve above shows how demand will fall as prices rise.

A further influence on share prices was resentment from the French. Many French people are concerned that their culture is being lost as American culture spreads. As the article says, Euro Disney could be a 'Cultural Chernobyl'. Bad publicity such as this and endless speculation on financial difficulties was bound to encourage shareholders to sell and the few buyers to pay lower prices for the shares. Euro Disney also lost the chance to get cash by selling land when property prices fell in Paris, and high interest rates were increasing their costs.

15

(iv) The alternative solutions are:

(1) Closing down.
(2) A rights issue.
(3) Attract more visitors in the winter months.
(4) Cut operating costs.
(5) Sales of assets such as hotels.
(6) Restructuring the package of debts.
(7) Improve efficiency and service.
(8) Becoming more French.
(9) Help from the parent company.

The first alternative will involve the loss of the huge sums already invested in the business. It could only be considered if market research showed the business was never going to be successful. Certainly in the short term, so long as revenues were higher than operating costs, it should stay in business. The loss would be greater if output was zero and no contribution was being made to fixed costs.

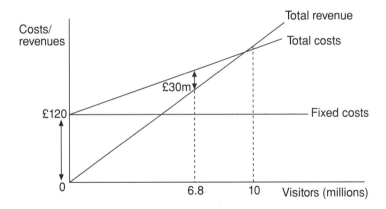

Using the above fictitious break-even chart, if the firm produces nothing it makes a loss of £120 million whereas it if has 6.8 million visitors the loss is only £30 million. Obviously this loss cannot go on forever and if, as I said earlier, that was predicted it should cut its losses and sell up.

The other plans could be lumped into two alternative financial plans as opposed to operating plans. It seems that the financial plans could be dangerous palliatives. Obtaining money from banks, shareholders or Walt Disney may just be putting off the evil day when the real problems the company faces must be tackled. On the other hand they could get the company over its temporary current difficulties. The forecasters may have worked out that when the recession is over and the property market picks up that Euro Disney will be profitable. Euro Disney needs to weigh up the costs and benefits of the different financial packages. Money from Walt Disney or shareholders will be cheaper than from banks, but there may be disadvantages in terms of loss of managerial control.

Some people would argue that getting the product right is the only real alternative. They can do nothing about the Parisian weather (maybe they should have chosen Spain) but they can influence the staff. They need to improve management and staff attitudes to provide good customer care. They need to provide what the customer wants. The French expect good restaurants and alcohol. They need to research the price elasticity of demand of all their merchandise, hotel accommodation and other packages. I have illustrated this by the following made-up examples.

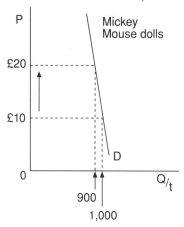
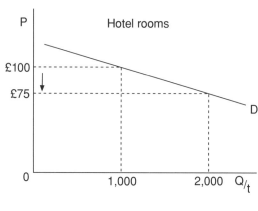

In the case of Mickey Mouse dolls they should raise their prices as demand is not very responsive (price-inelastic) and revenue rises from £10,000 to £18,000 despite demand falling. On the other hand they should lower their hotel prices as demand rises by a much greater percentage than price falls (price-elastic) and revenue rises from £100,000 to £150,000.

As well as trying to raise revenue they should continue to cut costs, particularly administration costs. In my view getting the product right is the long-term solution to their problems.   **15**

(b) (i) The product life cycle shows the different phases a product goes through from the start of its life to its death. When it is first introduced sales are low. If it is successful sales grow but eventually sales reach a maximum known as the mature stage. Sales begin to decline and the product may be withdrawn.

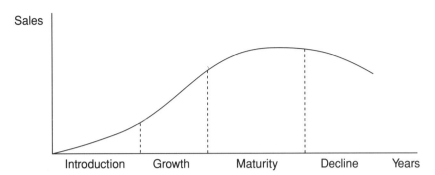

The length in time of a product life cycle varies from product to product.   **5**

(ii) Euro Disney will want to know the length of the theme park's product life cycle. If it is short they will have to recoup their investment quickly. They will want to know what phase of the cycle they are in. They must hope they are still in the introductory phase. If they are then they will adopt the appropriate pricing and promotion strategies, e.g. penetration pricing.

If they are in the decline phase then they will have to consider closure or extension strategies. In other words, the product life cycle is used in determining the marketing and overall company strategy.   **8**

(iii) They could employ different pricing strategies as discussed earlier. In particular they could put package deals together which included flights, accommodation, meal and entrance fees. These would have to be attractive enough to raise revenue. But they would also have to be profitable. Prices must be competitive with Disney World in Florida and other parks. Euro Disney may have to go for a complete relaunch in order to change its image and put the bad publicity behind it. Each of the 4Ps would have to be thought through in a coherent strategy.

The company has already changed the name of the theme park. 'Euro' has bad connotations for some, whereas Paris has romantic and quality associations. The product must be excellent. The staff must be highly trained and courteous. New rides which are more spectacular than those of competitors should be introduced. The park should emphasise French culture as this will be attractive to the French and other visitors. As prices must be too high because of competitors, 'high price/high quality' will not be the strategy. Instead reasonable prices producing good value for money may be the strategy. This would have to be emphasised in the promotion used. This could be targeted at families. They could use celebrities who appeal to children to promote visits so that the children pester their parents. They could place adverts in children's comics, during children's programmes and have special offers/competitions linked to Disney films/videos.   **15**

(c) (i) It may be that many of the management and administration jobs were linked with setting up the park and are no longer necessary. It is possible that they were over staffed due to forecasting their staffing needs incorrectly. It may be that they have identified efficiencies/economies of scale in their use of management. Perhaps they can make greater use of computers. The most likely rationale is that when forced to cut staff you cut staff behind the scenes so that visitors do not notice. Visitors want people on hand to look after their needs. A visitor having to wait for help would not be good for Euro Disney's reputation. In fact, surly staff have already been a problem. Disney want to be famous for having plenty of smiling, helpful attendants. It is also more difficult to replace this service by new technology.   **10**

(ii) I would issue an individual (though not personalised) notice to each member of staff. I think it should be sent to individuals as they each need a copy to refer to. It certainly should not appear on notice boards as that would cause resentment, confusion and rumours. I would not personalise it in case the individual thought they were being singled out. I would try and make it as courteous and non-threatening as possible.

Personnel Officer
Euro Disney
Paris

1st October 1995

Dear Colleague

I am writing to all the firm's employees to keep you informed of the staffing situation at Euro Disney.

As you know we are completing the transition from a start up organisation to a full operating company. This inevitably involves a small reduction in the size of the workforce. We have begun the consultation procedure with the staff's representatives. We have agreed to ask for 950 volunteers from the managerial and administrative staff to come forward to take voluntary redundancy. The terms are very generous including a £40,000 lump sum, a relocation package and job-finding help. Please call at the Personnel Office or see your staff representative for further details.
Yours sincerely

M. Moule
Personnel Officer

10

Examiner's tip

Though it was not asked for, this candidate gave a rationale for the draft statement. This showed the examiner the thinking behind the candidate's statement.

(iii) The size of the redundancy package will be a big influence. Benefits which are too small may not attract volunteers. The state of the job market is crucial. If the chances of getting another job are good then the redundancy payment is a bonus which can give an employee financial security. On the other hand it would be soon used up if no jobs are available. Employees' feelings about their work will affect their decision to volunteer. If they are unhappy they may jump at the chance. Similarly if they think Euro Disney will not last much longer, they may decide to jump ship while good terms are still available.

10

Mark scheme

5 **(a) (i)** Simple definitions   *2 × 2 marks*
              Explained in Euro Disney context   *2 × 4 marks*
       (ii) Just description   *1 mark*
              Notes same trend   *2–3 marks*
              Compares and explains   *4 marks*

(iii)	List of factors specific to Euro Disney	*1–3 marks*
	List of internal and external factors	*4–5 marks*
	Brief explanation	*6–7 marks*
	Well developed explanation with analysis	*8–12 marks*
	Analysis and evaluation	*13–15 marks*
(iv)	Lists alternative solutions	*1–3 marks*
	Explains and analyses alternatives	*4–7 marks*
	Evaluates alternatives fully	*8–15 marks*

(b) **(i)** Brief explanation   *1–2 marks*
        Full explanation /diagram   *3–5 marks*

     (ii) Brief explanation   *1–3 marks*
        Develops explanation in context   *4–8 marks*

    (iii) Brief explanation,
        Superficial notes on 4Ps   *1–3 marks*
        Full explanation of 4Ps in context   *4–7 marks*
        Analysis of marketing strategy   *8–11 marks*
        Analysis and evaluation   *12–15 marks*

(c) **(i)** Brief explanation   *1–3 marks*
        Develops explanation   *4–6 marks*
        Analysis of job-cutting programme   *7–8 marks*
        Analysis and evaluation   *9–10 marks*

     (ii) Partially thought out statement   *1–3 marks: poor format cannot get more than 2*
        Well explained statement   *4–7 marks*
        Courteous, reassuring, thorough statement   *8–10 marks*

    (iii) List of factors   *1–3 marks*
        Explanation of factors   *4–7 marks*
        Analysis of success   *8–10 marks*

                                Maximum 100 marks

4 ACCOUNTS AND FINANCE

Candidate's answer	Mark

1 Profit and loss statement, balance sheet, and a directors' report and auditors' report. **1**

2 FIFO stands for first in first out and LIFO stands for last in first out. It means in the first case that we assume the first stocks bought are the first stocks sold and therefore the remaining stocks are the more expensive stocks. **2**

3 A budgetary system allows the firm to keep control of costs and to forecast future expenses. Variance analysis can be used as a way of identifying problems within the business. **2**

4 (a) Depreciation is an accounting term used to show how the value of an asset such as a machine falls over time. It allocates the cost of the fall in value over the expected life of the machine. **3**

   (b) (i) Wear and tear.

       (ii) Technical obsolescence.

       (iii) Changes in fashion. **3**

   (c) £20,000 − £3,000 = £17,000.
      £17,000/5 = £3,400.
      So the annual depreciation is £3,400. **3**

Examiner's tip

Easy 3 marks as all the information is contained in the question.

   (d) The straight-line method is easy to calculate and easy to understand. The book value of an asset declines by an equal amount each year. The reducing balance method is more complex to calculate. Because the asset declines by a percentage, the book value of an asset declines more rapidly after it is first bought. This may be more realistic as we all know from our purchase of cars. It may also be more sensible than the straight-line method as the cost of an asset may be more evenly spread if you combine a smaller depreciation expense with the greater cost of repair and maintenance as an asset gets older. **6**

   (e) See attached graph.

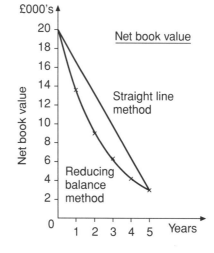

7

(f) Depreciation varies according to the method used. There is no actual outflow of cash from the business but profits are reduced to allow for the future replacement of the asset in the future. **3**

Mark scheme

4 (a) Sound definition includes that it is financial not physical. A way of spreading the cost of an asset and finding its value.   *3 × 1 marks*

  (b) Time, technical developments, changing market conditions.   *3 × 1 marks*

  (c) Straight Line Method = (original value – residual value)/estimated life: £17,000/5 = £3,400.   *3 × 1 marks*

  (d) Answers include:
Straight Line Method is easier to use, same amount deducted each year.
Reducing Balance Method more difficult, higher depreciation at first, more sensible.
LEVEL 1
Identifies main features.   *1–3 marks*
LEVEL 2
Makes comparison.   *4–6 marks*

  (e) 1 mark for each normal graph requirement e.g. labels, titles, scales.   *max 7 marks*

  (f) Explanation of accounting conventions.   *3 × 1 marks*

                                                  Maximum 25 marks

---

5 (a) $279.7 \div 2{,}843.2 \times 100 = 9.84\%$.   **2**

  (b) Earnings per share includes all profits, and some profits are retained in the business. Dividends are only those which are distributed.   **2**

  (c) The percentage increase in profits has been greater than the percentage increase in sales, therefore the margin must be increased.   **2**

  (d) (i) Ratios for one year tell us very little. We should look at a company's performance over five years to see the trend.

     (ii) One firm's ratios are not very useful. We should compare them to other similar firms to see if they are doing as well as other firms.

     (iii) Accountants often use bench-mark figures to enable judgments to be made.   **6**

  (e) (i) Vertical integration enables a company to secure supplies or retail outlets.

     (ii) Horizontal integration is where a company takes over competitors to either increase monopoly power or gain economies of scale.

     (iii) Lateral integration is where a company takes over another company not closely related. The prime motive is diversification.   **6**

Mark scheme

5 **(a)** 279.7/ 2843.2 × 100 = 9.8%. *2 marks*

(b) Earnings per share includes all profits i.e. retained profits as well as dividend. *2 marks*

(c) Trading profit has risen 22.2% compared to sales which have risen 19.4%. *2 marks*

(d) Includes: intercompany comparisons, comparisons over time, use of benchmarks.
LEVEL 1
Identifies factors. *1–3 marks*
LEVEL 2
Explains factors. *4–6 marks*

(e) Vertical – backward to suppliers or forward to retailers.
Horizontal – take over competitors.
Lateral – increased profit, spreads risks, makes safer.
LEVEL 1
Defines integration. *1–3 marks*
LEVEL 2
Explains reasons. *4–6 marks*

Maximum 18 marks

---

6 **(a)** Buys cars at £2,300 buys 14 a month:
£2,300 × 14 = £32,200.

Sells cars at £3,000, sells 12 a month:
£3,000 × 12 = £36,000.
£36,000 − £32,200 = £3,800. **3**

Examiner's tip

All the information is in the case. Set out your calculations clearly.

(b)

	June	July	August	September
Balance brought forward	(15)	(15.7)	(37.4)	(58.1)
Normal sales	36	36	36	36
Contract sales	0	0	0	30
Cash in	21	20.3	(1.4)	7.9
Wages	(2.5)	(2.5)	(2.5)	(2.75)
Overheads	(2.0)	(3.0)	(2.0)	(2.0)
Normal purchases	(32.2)	(32.2)	(32.2)	(32.2)
Contract purchases	0	(20.0)	(20.0)	(20.0)
Cash out	(36.7)	(57.7)	(56.7)	(56.95)
Balance carried forward	(15.7)	(37.4)	(58.1)	(49.05)

10

Assumptions

(1) Normal sales per month.

(2) Buys 5 contract cars at £4,000 each, starting in July.

(3) Overheads same as respective months the previous year.

(4) Wages rise by 10% in September.

(5) Sells contract cars at £5,000 each, receives first 20% of revenue in September. **3**

Maria is right that the firm's cash flow will be difficult for the next few months. **2**

Examiner's tip

The candidate has done all that was asked for in the question. The cash flow forecast is excellent and based on clear assumptions. It is good to see brackets being used to indicate negative values.

(c) As his bank manager, I would be concerned about Spiro's cash flow problems, especially in view of his already having a £50,000 overdraft. I would be worried about the viability and reliability of the contract sales. Knowing the area of town that Spiro's business is located in, I would doubt his ability to move up market. I would be concerned about the lack of business expertise in the firm, though Maria's knowledge is an asset. The sales of cars are very dependent on the state of the economy and on interest rates. If Spiro's normal sales fall during a recession, would Spiro meet his commitments to the bank? If the worst came to the worst, what collateral could the bank rely on? **12**

(d) Spiro lacks business skills, which is typical of small firms. Spiro and Ron were over-worked before George's arrival, which is a normal difficulty of a sole trader. A sole trader often has to carry out many different roles. Sole traders often rely on very limited markets which might be quite vulnerable. They often experience cash flow problems. They are often short of capital. They lack access to financial institutions. In my judgment this means they are much more likely to go out of business than a large firm. Large firms can spread their risks so that if one product falls in demand it is counterbalanced by another product doing well. They have access to funds on the stock market or from institutions such as merchant banks. They are able to use their power to gain lower interest rates, favourable discounts, etc. In comparison, Spiro's interest payments and supplier costs are higher. **10**

(e) Spiro certainly should consult Maria at an early stage. He should be more systematic about the way he makes decisions. He and Maria should thoroughly think out the aims for the business. They should seek expert advice. All in all they should employ better planning. Spiro does seem to make decisions in an arbitrary fashion, without looking at the consequences. For example, he is giving a 10% pay rise as a way of motivating George – he should look at alternative methods. He should have thought about the problem of the three months' outlay on the contract cars before any revenue came in. If Spiro is going to move up market, he, Maria and their advisers should be sure it is a sound long-term aim. They should then devise a strategy based on market research. This way involves changes in location, in the type of cars bought, in their prices, and in the way they are promoted. His business plan would have to convince the bank manager. **10**

Examiner's tip

The candidate has made excellent use of the information in the case. They have applied their knowledge of business studies in a very convincing way.

Mark scheme

6 (a) Buying in 14 at £2,300 = £32,200.   *1 mark*

Selling 12 at £3,000 = $\dfrac{£36,000}{£3,800}$ *1 mark*
                                                                                          1 mark

(b)

	June	*July*	*August*	*September*
Opening balance	(15)	(15.7)	(37.4)	(58.1)
Usual sales	36.0	36	36.0	36.0
Contract sales	0	0	0	30.0
CASH IN	21.0	20.3	(1.4)	7.9
Wages	(2.5)	(2.5)	(2.5)	(2.75)
Overheads	(2.0)	(3.0)	(2.0)	(2.0)
Usual purchases	(32.2)	(32.2)	(32.2)	(32.2)
Contract purchases	0	(20.0)	(20.0)	(20.0)
CASH OUT	(36.7)	(57.7)	(56.7)	(56.95)
Overdraft	(15.7)	(37.4)	(58.1)	(49.05)

10 marks

Cash flow
1 mark for each correct calculation which involved making decision/identifying changes.

Assumptions
Answers include: costs stay the same, increase in wages, usual sales constant.   *3 marks*

Explains why Maria was right.   *2 marks*

(c) Answers could include:
Lack of management experience.
Lack of security.
Present site.
Size of current overdraft.
Economic conditions.

LEVEL 1
Identified factors from the case.   *1–3 marks*

LEVEL 2
Explained 3 factors from the case.   *4–6 marks*

LEVEL 3
Analyses factors.   *7–9 marks*

LEVEL 4
Offered an evaluated argument for granting or not granting Spiro's request.

10–12 marks

(d) Answers might include:
Lack of management training.
Carrying out all management functions.
Lack of access to finances.
Reliance on one major contract.
Problems with cash flow.
Financial insecurity.
Lack of cover for staff.
Impact of bigger firms.

LEVEL 1
Knowledge-based answer.   *1–2 marks*

LEVEL 2
Applies knowledge to case study.   *3–6 marks*

LEVEL 3
Explains and analyses difficulties.   *7–8 marks*

LEVEL 4
Detailed evaluation of difficulties.   *9–10 marks*

(e) Answers may include:
  –   Using Maria's expertise
  –   Forward planning
  –   Relocating
  –   Cash flow management
  –   Market niche
  –   Try new business

LEVEL 1
Identifies sound pieces of advice.   *1–3 marks*

LEVEL 2
Analyses advice.   *4–7 marks*

LEVEL 3
Produces coherent strategy.   *8–10 marks*

                                                                    Maximum 50 marks

5 PRODUCTION

Candidate's answer	Mark

1 High costs for raw materials, costs of inspection. **2**

2 Vertical integration is taking over a firm that produces the same product but at a different stage of production. Horizontal expansion is taking over a firm that makes the same product at the same stage of production. **2**

3 (i) In case of increased demand.
(ii) In order to transport in bulk.
(iii) In case there was a shortage of supply. **3**

4 (i) Increases in average costs.
(ii) Industrial relations problems. **2**

Mark scheme

1 Cost of labour, cost of raw materials, quality control. *2 × 1*

2 Vertical expansion is taking over firms closer to the market or raw materials.
Horizontal expansion is taking over firms to increase market share or control. *2 × 1*

3 In case of increase in demand, failure of supply, inflation, to ensure steady production. *3 × 1*

4 Poor industrial relations, poor decision making, increase in long-run average costs, lack of management control. *2 × 1*

---

5 **(a)** **(i)** Q = 10,000, total revenue = £500,000, therefore price = £50.
Q = 10,000, total variable cost = £250,000, therefore average variable cost = £25.
At Q = 13,000 Total revenue = £650,000
            Total cost = £575,000
            <u>Profit = £75,000</u> **4**

   (ii) Contribution is price – AVC. If P = 45 and AVC = £25 then contribution = £20. Fixed costs of £250,000/20 gives a break-even output of 12,500, therefore the margin of safety is now only 500 and has <u>changed by 2,500</u>. **2**

   (iii) Break-even charts are fairly simplistic, assuming that sales do not change as price changes. They also assume that a firm can sell all of its output. **2**

> **Examiner's tip**
>
> Clearly set out with the final answer underlined. The candidate spotted that the question asked for the change in the margin of safety.

   (b) Costs incurred during production, e.g. raw materials, which can be attributed directly to the product. The difference in prices at each stage are due to the costs of the different firms involved and their mark-up for profit. **4**

   (c) The advantages to Smellies are that they only have to sell to the wholesaler rather than to lots of stores, which could reduce their distribution costs as they do not have to transport small amounts to many firms but a large amount to Cosgraves. It also means that Cosgraves incur the cost of holding stocks, rather than them. It may be the case that Cosgraves have better knowledge of retailers than Smellies. The disadvantages to Smellies are that they lose some control of how the product gets to the retailer, and that the price to the retailer will be higher because of the wholesaler's profit margin. **5**

Examiner's tip

Several points are made because 5 marks are available. Knowledge is applied sensibly.

(d) As there are lots of soaps on the market, Smellies need to make themselves distinctive, which is a major function of branding. Firms try to create brand loyalty, which is useful if they have to raise prices or launch new products with the same brand name. Brands can become very important to a firm and have recently started to appear on balance sheets as an asset. **4**

(e) Smellies could accept Cosgrave's complaint and introduce more quality control measures of their own. More likely, they could argue that one bar being discoloured out of two thousand delivered is not an acceptable reason for returning the batch. They need to argue that the sample is not statistically valid and that Cosgraves should take a larger sample. **4**

Examiner's tip

The statistical reference is important.

Mark scheme

5 (a) (i) Price = £50 = £500,000/10,000
AVC = £25 = £250,000/10,000
Current profit = TR of £650,000 less TVC of £325,000 less TFC of £250,000 = £75,000 *4 marks*

(ii) Present margin of safety = 3,000
New price = £45
New break-even = 250,000/20 = 12,500
New margin of safety is 3,000 – 2,500 = 500. *2 marks*

(iii) Assumes all products sold. Assumes prices/cost do not change as output changes. *2 marks*

(b) Direct costs are the same as variable costs. They can be attributed to particular goods e.g. raw material cost. Economies of scale, profit margins, price inelastic. *4 marks*

(c) Advantages: specialist function, reduces cost of holding stock, transport costs. Disadvantages: wholesalers' profits, lack of contact with retailers. *5 marks*

(d) Creates unique selling proposition. Recognition of firm. Brand image. Creation of portfolio. *4 marks*

(e) Comment on size of sample. May be one-off batch. May not reflect rest of the batch. *4 marks*

Maximum 25 marks

6 **(a)** A large company owns all the shares in a small company. **2**

(b) **(i)** Because of the presence of other firms that they work in close collaboration with, this would have benefits to both companies, e.g. transport costs would be lower. It would be easy to arrange meetings between companies.

(ii) As a specialist engineering firm they would require specialist labour and certainly appreciate the advantage of a specialist engineering pool in the area. This would make recruitment easier. They may even be able to pay lower wages.

(iii) Aston Science Park would have the kind of facility that a firm like Stocklin would need. They are a specialist firm who need expert advice and facilities. Aston will have the technology they require. Being close at hand would reduce costs to the firm. **9**

Examiner's tip

The three reasons are given in the article. However, to gain 9 marks the points must be developed.

(c) It may be important to the firm for legal reasons. It may be against the law to sell products that do not conform to the standards. Even if it is not illegal, many of its customers will insist on conforming to standards. Thus it is important in terms of making sales. As a firm that wants to sell throughout Europe, European standards would be useful in terms of producing uniform products to ease production and gain economies of scale. They could use the standards as a marketing advantage over non-European firms. **7**

(d) One advantage is easy retrieval of documents. By being computerised, the documents may be accessed in a very short time and accurately. Another major advantage is that being held in one place they are likely to be more secure and not cost as much to keep secure.

A significant disadvantage would be the initial cost of automation. It may require a new building and expensive machinery. Another disadvantage would be the potential for computer failure and therefore of not being able to access any documents at times. **8**

Mark scheme

6 **(a)** All shares owned by Stocklin. *2 marks*

(b) Near collaborating company/understand each other/complex product/needs experts/near source of specialist engineers/quality is its main reason for success/Aston offers wide range of services/Science Park close to University/city contains banks, etc./Birmingham communications good/plenty of local suppliers/easy access for workers/access to EU market/UK low-wage economy. *3 × 3 marks*

(c) Standards can be a barrier to trade/EU standards overcome this/customers will seek known standards/improves marketing/legal requirement.
For max marks need to show importance to Stocklin – 7 marks

(d) Economies of scale/one building/one management and staff/cheaper to run/no duplication/control and accuracy/fast and efficient/security.
Systems break down/poor communications from branches/expensive to set up/lack of human touch/customers having to wait. *4 × 2 marks*
Maximum 26 marks

7 (a) <u>Current ratio</u>

Current assets : Current liabilities

£155,000 : £82,000   1.89 : 1

As a ratio of 2 : 1 is regarded as safe this may be a little low.

<u>Acid Test Ratio</u>

Current assets less stock : Current liabilities

70,000 : 82,000   0.85 : 1

A ratio of 1 : 1 is the normal benchmark and this is very worrying.

<u>Gearing</u>

$\frac{150,000}{168,000}$ = 89%. This is worryingly high.

The club is in a difficult financial situation.   **5**

Examiner's tip

This is a good answer. The candidate uses sensible ratios and makes comments on them.

(b) If it was not possible to turn the stock into cash then the club may not be able to meet its liabilities. The stock a football club has is probably not easily turned into cash in the way a shop would. Not being able to pay creditors may lead to them refusing to supply goods in the short term. Worse still, in the medium term, they may force the club into receivership. Similar actions may take place with the tax authorities or with the bank. The club's bank in the short term might refuse to increase their overdraft. In the medium term they may demand repayment of the whole overdraft. It may be difficult to pay the players and other staff. They may lose players. It may be impossible to pay for ground improvements.   **8**

Examiner's tip

To gain more than half marks both medium- and long-term problems must be addressed.

(c) As stated in the answer to part (a), the club is very highly geared. This means it will be paying very high interest charges. If it is profitable this may be satisfactory as it means ownership of the club is not shared with many shareholders. However, in a risky business like football, high gearing is very dangerous.   **3**

Examiner's tip

The candidate's knowledge of theory has been appropriately applied.

(d) In the short term I would recommend converting stocks and debtors into cash in order to be able to reduce the bank overdraft. If the club has any valuable players it may have to sell them. In the long term the club should consider issuing more shares in order to reduce the gearing of the club. This has the disadvantage of reducing existing shareholders' control but will be much less risky than not being able to meet the term loan repayments. I would also recommend putting the value of the players into the balance sheet as many Premiership clubs are beginning to do.   **4**

Mark scheme

7 **(a)** LEVEL 1
Set out correct formula ratios.   *1–2 marks*
LEVEL 2
Correct calculations plus comment.   *3–5 marks*

(b) LEVEL 1
Identifies possible problems.   *1–2 marks*
LEVEL 2
Explains possible problems.   *3–4 marks*
LEVEL 3
Analyses possible problems and distinguishes between short and medium term.
5–8 marks

(c) LEVEL 1
Calculates gearing.   *1 mark*
LEVEL 2
Explains significance of the club's gearing ratios.   *2–3 marks*

(d) LEVEL 1
Makes recommendations.   *1–2 marks*
LEVEL 2
Explains recommendations.   *3–4 marks*
Maximum 20 marks

6 THE EXTERNAL ENVIRONMENT

Candidate's answer	Mark

1 (i) The high cost of housing.

(ii) Lack of skills.   **2**

2 A fall in the value of the pound raises import prices which will increase the firm's raw material costs and may force it to raise prices. On the other hand, the price of exports will fall, which may enable the firm to be more competitive abroad.   **4**

3 (i) 1974 Employment Protection Act.

(ii) 1974 Health and Safety at Work Act.

(iii) 1970 Equal Pay Act.   **3**

4 High-level unemployment reduces people's incomes and therefore could reduce demand for manufactured products. On the other hand, with a pool of unemployed labour it may be possible to employ workers at lower wages.   **2**

Mark scheme

1 Any 2 correct geographic or occupational barriers to mobility.   *2 marks*

2 Devaluation raises import prices and lowers export prices; may export more.   *4 marks*

3 HASWA, TURER, TUPE, etc.   *3 marks*

4 Lower wages, pool of labour, stable workforce, sales revenue low.   *2 marks*

---

5 (a) BP are trying to illustrate that the tax goes to the Government and not to them. It is a high proportion of the cost and, if removed, prices have not risen significantly. Similarly, inflation, which is a general rise in prices, means that all products have risen, not just petrol. As the value of money falls, the price BP gains does not buy as much. If we use constant prices then, according to BP, petrol prices have not risen since 1969.   **10**

(b) (i) VAT is a tax charged at a percentage of the price of the product. Excise duty is a specific tax per unit. Both of them are indirect taxes, i.e. charged on purchases of products. In some ways they are a hidden tax in that customers are paying them to sellers rather than direct to the Government. The seller is collecting the tax for the Government.   **4**

(ii) As you can see from the diagram below, the effect of VAT is to shift the supply curve upwards and to the left. This raises the price of the product and because demand is inelastic does not reduce demand significantly, so the Government gains a great deal of revenue. The two supply curves diverge because, as VAT is a percentage tax, the actual monetary amount of tax paid increases as price increases.   **6**

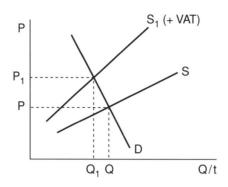

(c) (i) Oil is priced in dollars on the world markets and even within the UK by many firms. If a barrel of oil cost $18 and the rate of exchange was $1.80:£1 then the price of a barrel would be £10. If sterling rose to $2:£1 then the $18 barrel would cost only £9. In other words, a rise in the sterling exchange rate should lead to a fall in the UK domestic price.

(ii) If we apply the above example to a range of products, we can see that an appreciation of the exchange rate should lower UK inflation. A depreciation or devaluation would lead to inflation which could easily set off wage price-inflation.

(iii) The price of petrol will be one of the factors influencing the retail price index. In addition, transport costs are important to both businesses and consumers and therefore there would be a significant impact on UK inflation. **15**

(d) A fall in the price of petrol should lead to an increase in demand for petrol and therefore to increase use of cars, lorries, etc. This will have beneficial effects on the motor car industry and on road haulage firms, both of which may employ more people. This could lead to multiplier effects in the economy. As car workers' incomes rise they spend more, raising the income of other firms. These firms take on more workers, leading to a general recovery. This will be helped by many firms' profits rising due to the fall of their transport costs. However, there are disadvantages. It may further encourage the transfer from rail to road, damaging British Rail's income. Environmentalists may become very concerned at the amount of pollution. Many road users may become very concerned at the increased congestion on the roads. **15**

Mark scheme

5 (a) LEVEL 1
Simple definitions. *1–3 marks*

LEVEL 2
Explains concepts. *4–7 marks*

LEVEL 3
Analyses statement. *8–10 marks*

(b) (i) Specific versus ad valorem tax. Explains that it is indirect, and collected by the retailer. *4 marks*

(ii) LEVEL 1
Diagram. *1–3 marks*

LEVEL 2
Diagram and explanation. *4–6 marks*

(c) (i) Answers include: oil paid for in dollars, therefore affected by exchange rate.

(ii) Fall in sterling raises import prices and inflation.

(iii) Petrol major expenditure for many households.

LEVEL 1
Superficial knowledge. *1–2 marks*

LEVEL 2
Explains clearly. *3–5 marks*

(d) Answers include: micro-economic effects on road and rail industry; macro-economic effects: positive multiplier, fall in inflation.

LEVEL 1
Superficial ideas. *1–4 marks*

LEVEL 2
Explains ideas. *5–9 marks*

LEVEL 3
Analysis benefits and statements leading to evaluation. *10–15 marks*

Maximum 50 marks

---

6 (a) (i) The major external factor which influenced David's business was the remarks by the junior government minister. Whether the eggs were contaminated with salmonella or not was irrelevant, the bad publicity had a damaging effect. Consumers believed the remarks and therefore stopped buying the eggs. This put downward pressure on David's sales and prices. This therefore reduced David's revenue and meant there was a danger of not being able to cover costs.

(ii) David had also been influenced by the closure of the South Wales coal mine in which he worked and the lack of opportunities in the area. This led to his and Maggie's decision to move to Bristol. This illustrates how the state of the economy and government policy affects firms. It also shows how different regions of the country will have different levels of prosperity. This leads to migration between the regions, just as David and Maggie did.

(iii) They were also influenced by the attitude of local residents. They had been upset by the behaviour of the previous owner, by the smell, the unsightly buildings and the noisy lorries. In the case study this appears only to cause

David and Maggie to sympathise with the residents. However, it could cause a loss of local sales and objections to future planning requests. As animal rights issues become more popular it could cause locals to join protests if the farm uses battery farming techniques, as I have assumed from my reading of the case study.

(iv) David's business has benefited from his local bank manager's attitude. Many good ideas from prospective entrepreneurs never get off the ground as they fail to get finance because of the timidity of a bank manager. David on the other hand was able to expand because both he and his bank manager were confident there would be a worthwhile return on the investment.

(v) Changing social attitudes also had an impact on the farm. Consumers were becoming more health conscious, which meant eating fewer fried breakfasts. This meant a fall in egg sales and therefore tougher competitive conditions for David's business, though he was convinced he could survive until less efficient egg producers went bankrupt and prices recovered. **10**

Examiner's tip

This is an excellent answer. One important point is to make it easy for the Examiner to mark. Unlike with some candidates, it is clear which question and which part of the question is being answered. This candidate also numbers the five factors which have affected the business. In terms of content they gain marks by making use of the case study. They gain the second mark for each of the five points by analysing the factor drawn from the case.

(b) <u>1988 revenue</u>

The original 1,000 hens lay 1.5 eggs a day on average, which equals 1,500 per day.

1,500/12 = 125 dozen per day
x 365
= 45,625 dozen for the year.

Assuming (as David and his bank manager did in paragraph 7) a price of 46p per dozen and that all output will be sold:

= £20,987.50 per year for original flock

plus half a year with an extra 1,000 hens adds 50% to the revenue

  £20,987.50
+ £10,493.75
= <u>£31,481.25</u>

<u>1988 costs</u>

<u>Variable costs</u>

For the whole year David had 1,000 hens. They cost £11.70 per 100 per week in running costs.

10 × £11.70 × 52 = £6,084

Plus 1,000 more hens for 26 weeks is £3,042

Total running costs are therefore <u>£9,126</u>.

Buying the extra 1,000 hens cost £200 per 100, therefore the purchase cost is <u>£2,000</u>.

<u>Fixed costs</u>

The fixed costs are given in the question as £6,200. This figure assumes a great deal about depreciation, interest rates and slaughtering. It does not take into account selling the extra 1,000 birds for slaughter in December. However, as it is given in the question it is the figure I will use.

<u>Total costs</u>

Total costs are £9,126 + £2,000 + £6,200 = <u>£17,326</u>

<u>Total profit</u>

Profit is total revenue less total costs

£31,481.25 − £17,326 = **£14,155.25**

Even if the crisis had not occurred David would have failed to achieve his personal target of £15,000 profit, but not by too much.   **10**

Examiner's tip

This is an excellent answer. The candidate has set out their work clearly. They would have gained marks for method even if the calculations had been wrong. They gain more marks for providing a correct answer and stating a conclusion. They also gain marks for stating that assumptions are being made and that there is therefore an element of uncertainty.

(c) David is facing a very difficult period during which his ability to cope with the crisis, compared with that of his competitors, will determine his survival. He must take advice from many quarters and weigh up all the information he gathers.

He has to decide if the rumours of government action are true or not. If the Government are going to offer substantial compensation, he may not have to take much action.

He has to judge whether the adverse publicity will have a long-term effect. If it does he may have to consider alternative uses for the farm. If it is only a short-term problem he may able to ride out the storm.

This is influenced by another factor, namely the attitude of his bank manager. He will need to seek his advice on help in sustaining any losses.

This will again be affected by the behaviour of other egg producers. If many of them leave the industry, David and the bank may see this as a long-term opportunity. It may be worth putting up with low prices and sales for good profits when the market and price recover.

If the market is not going to recover it would be best to act immediately. He will get a better price when sending the birds for slaughter if he sends them before too many other producers do the same.

This also has the advantage of saving on the running costs of the hens, which would reduce his losses as he may not be able to sell the eggs at a price above costs, if at all.   **10**

Examiner's tip

The candidate has made many telling points. Importantly, each point has been developed, explaining its significance. This enables them to gain development marks. The first few lines also illustrate that factors will have to be evaluated against each other.

(d) Firms vary in their behaviour, just like people generally. Some behave well naturally and some only if they are forced to. The main element of force is <u>the law</u>. In the case study the previous owner had built hen-houses which his neighbours regarded as eyesores. Tougher planning rules would stop such behaviour. Many people believe that out-of-town shopping centres are damaging the environment by destroying the countryside and causing increased use of cars. This too is being halted by stricter interpretation of the planning laws by the present Secretary of State for the Environment.

The Government is influenced by <u>social attitudes</u>. As people have become more environmentally conscious they have put more pressure on firms. Similarly, the people who own or work in firms will reflect social norms. David and Maggie may themselves become concerned with their treatment of their hens. This may lead them to switch from battery farming techniques to free-range methods. An example of this in the wider world has been Anita Roddick and The Body Shop. The success of her company has shown that altruism can be combined with making profits.

It is also the case that <u>pressure groups</u> can force firms to change even when they might lose profits. If animal rights activists started picketing David's farm he might give in to their demands. Certainly the cross-channel ferry companies gave up the lucrative business of transporting live animals in response to pressure group activity.

On the other hand, it may have been the adverse <u>publicity</u> in the press which caused the change in behaviour. The companies may have felt this publicity would lead to fewer families being prepared to use the ferries. That would lead to a loss of revenue which might outweigh the revenue gained from transporting live animals.

Many firms have been accused of exploiting their workers and not having due regard to their health and safety. Sensible firms realise that the cost of looking after their workers is more than compensated by the greater productivity of a happy workforce. However, some firms will not incur costs unless they are forced to by trade union action.

10

Examiner's tip

The question is not clear whether the examples have to be drawn from the case or businesses generally. So the candidate has sensibly done both. They have obviously worked through past paper questions and learnt that the last question on the case study tends to be more wide ranging. Marks are awarded for examples and they always help illustrate a point. They have also underlined key words to bring them to the attention of the Examiner.

Mark scheme

6 (a) Answers may include:

European Union directives   Interest rates
Friendly bank manager   Local rules
Health consciousness   Government action
Junior minister's statements Impact of salmonella outbreak
Prices of supplies

LEVEL 1
Relevant points made superficially.   *1–3 marks*

LEVEL 2
Analyses points.   *4–7 marks*

LEVEL 3
Evaluation of points. *8–10 marks*

(b) <u>1988 revenue:</u>
1,000 birds   × 1.5 eggs/day
= 1,500 eggs/day
or 125 doz/day
× 365
= 45,625 doz/year × 46p per dozen
= £20,987.50 per year for the original flock
plus half year   <u>£10,493.75</u> for new flock
£31,481.25

<u>1988 costs:</u>
Buying | £2,000
Running costs
New flock £117 × 26 =   £3,042
Old flock   £6,084
Fixed costs   <u>£6,200</u>
Total costs   £17,326

<u>1988 profit:</u>
£31,481.25 – £17,326 = <u>£14,155.25</u>

LEVEL 1
Correct method. *1–3 marks*

LEVEL 2
Correct calculations. *4–7 marks*

LEVEL 3
States assumptions and draws conclusions. *8–10 marks*

(c) Answers include: Government aid; price falls; cost savings; is his flock infected?; ability to survive; alternative occupations.

LEVEL 1
Identifies reasons. *1–3 marks*

LEVEL 2
Analyses reasons. *4–7 marks*

LEVEL 3
Evaluates reasons. *8–10 marks*

(d) Answers include: Government action; legislation; media; environmental pressure groups; changing public attitudes. *10 marks*

Maximum 40 marks

---

7 (a) (i) A moving average is used to smooth out fluctuations in data so that trends are easier to see. **1**

(ii) 3 months are added together then divided by 3 to give an average. The next month the first of the 3 months drops out of the average and the current 3 months are totalled then divided by 3 to give the new average. **3**

(b) (i) Retail sales are fairly stable/flat. For the past 18 months there has been a slight but steady recovery, though they are only marginally higher than June 1990.

Manufacturing output collapsed from June 1990 to January 1992. It has bumped along the bottom since then but at least it has not fallen further.
Retail sales have recovered sooner and more substantially than manufacturing.   **6**

(ii) Both industrial production and manufacturing output are still in recession compared to June 1990, but after a bumpy start industrial production has steadily improved since January 1992. Manufacturing output has had two upturns a the beginning and end of 1992, being rather sluggish in between. A steady recovery seems possible and did in fact happen in 1993.   **3**

(c) Firstly, consumers may buy products from abroad leading to balance of payments problems. Secondly, demand may outstrip supply leading to inflationary pressures.
In response to both possibilities the Government may raise interest rates, which could kill the recovery before it begins.   **4**

(d) The economic factors described are almost the ideal combination for exports. The fall in the value of the pound will lead to a fall in the price of exports, making them more competitive abroad. They were already gaining a competitive edge from lower unit labour costs.
The firms may benefit from increased revenue if the demand for their products is price elastic. They may also be able to increase their profit margins if they do not pass on their cost gains to customers.   **4**

Mark scheme

7 **(a) (i)** To eliminate short-term fluctuations or highlight the trend of the data or calculate/identify seasonal variations.   *1 mark*

   (ii) Take an arithmetic mean of the first three months' data and then do the same for months two to four, three to five and so on.
   Up to 3 marks for such an explanation or for a correctly worked example.
   Notion of average over three months – 1 mark.

   (b) (i) Data shows decline in late 1990.
   Data shows recovery in 1992.
   Slight decline in retail sales relative to manufacturing
   Recovery in retail sales one year before manufacturing.
   Retail sales end two points higher.
   Manufacturing output ends about six points lower.
   Recovery is 'retail led'.
   Decline of manufacturing base.
   Purchase of imports boosts retail sales.
   Simple non-trend description of data. 1–2 marks
   Trend analysis (3–4 marks, for 4 marks look at both sets of data)
   Comparisons, possible causes, retail-led argument. 5–6 marks

   (ii) 1 × 2 marks for describing changes in each set of data.
   Third mark for overall comment/judgment which could include what has happened since.   *3 marks*

   (c) Answers may include:
   Increasing imports of finished goods: loss of home market.
   Inflationary pressure: deflationary government policies, loss of export markets.
   Balance of payments problems: government corrective action.
   Lack of productive capacity.

Low business confidence: lag over investment.

Recovery could be short lived: fickle consumers.

One mark for each relevant danger identified and a further
mark for development – 4 marks

(d) Declining exchange rate, leaving ERM, improved productivity, declining wage growth are set out in the text.

The likely benefits include:

Improving price competitiveness – depends on price elasticity.

Greater sales and consequent economies of scale – expect possible lag.

Room to improve quality, after-sales service etc. without compromising price.

Stable/lower interest rates – lower costs.

Increased profit margin – lower cost but stable prices.

One mark for each benefit identified and a further mark for development – 4 marks

Maximum 21 marks

---

8 (a) Customer reaction is very important. Many people prefer to eat and drink using crockery. They may decide not to use McDonald's unless it uses crockery. They may also feel that the quality of service is better if crockery is present. Having said the above, this appears to be an argument that was lost some time ago. Before McDonald's came to Britain, fast food restaurants did use crockery and therefore McDonald's may have been concerned that their decision not to may have been risky. However, McDonald's have proved to be very successful. So, either few customers actually care or customers felt the good things about McDonald's outweighed this problem.

From McDonald's point of view the savings in terms of less labour for clearing and washing up and in not having to buy crockery must outweigh any possible loss of custom.

But in the future, environmental concerns may change the balance of the argument. If customers are worried that polystyrene and paper cups damage the environment, they may stop eating at McDonald's.

A good decision in one moral climate may become a poor decision as views about what is ethical change. In terms of costs, speed of service and children friendliness, crockery would not help McDonald's. However, profits are the crucial issue. If the potential fall in revenue due to not using crockery was greater than the increased cost of using it, then McDonald's should use crockery. The McDonald's Fact Sheet 2 certainly shows that the firm believes customers are concerned with the environment and that it is in McDonald's interest to remove CFCs from their packaging. **10**

Examiner's tip

Arguments for and against have been put, the candidates sensibly use their own knowledge and experience.

(b) The Personnel Director will be very concerned about the staffing implications. Use of crockery may cause a big increase in staffing. It would have training implications. There may be health and safety considerations. The speed and standard of service may fall. Those staff who spend hours washing up may lose job satisfaction, and staff might have to be paid more.

The Financial Director will certainly be concerned if there are increases in staffing costs. There will also be the cost of buying the crockery and replacing the regular breakages. This will be balanced against not having to buy foam packaging and being able to re-use the crockery. If using crockery slows down the service then revenue will be affected. Both the Personnel and Finance Director will be concerned with the effect on costs and revenue and hence on profits. **10**

Examiner's tip

The candidate has decided that the marks would be divided between consideration of finance and personnel.

(c) As Managing Director I would want the board to stick to foam packaging. I believe crockery would not fit in with the McDonald's image and style. The main customer base is young people or families with young children. Teenagers may find crockery old-fashioned, being associated with more formal restaurants. Parents with young children want to be able to relax knowing the children cannot break anything, possibly hurting themselves, embarrassing the parents or costing them money.

However, the decision has to be based on market research. If customer views change from those outlined above, the decision will change. As Managing Director, I believe the customer is king and that we must meet the customer needs. **6**

Examiner's tip

The Managing Director would take a strategic view. Without saying it directly the candidate is implying that the decision must fit in with McDonald's USP – unique selling proposition.

Mark scheme

8 **(a)** Maximum five marks if only considers either customers or interests of firm.

Brief points	*1–2 marks*
Develops explanation of one point	*3–5 marks*
Develops explanation of more than one point	*6–7 marks*
Analysis of arguments	*8–10 marks*

(b) Maximum of five marks if only personnel or only finance.

Brief points	*1–2 marks*
Develops explanation of one point	*3–5 marks*
Develops explanation of more than one point	*6–7 marks*
Analysis of arguments	*8–10 marks*

(c)

Brief points	*1–2 marks*
Develops explanation	*3–4 marks*
Analysis of decision	*5–6 marks*

Maximum 26 marks

7 DECISION MAKING

Candidate's answer	Mark

1 (a) (i) Option 1 has £100,000 investment depreciated at 10% giving £10,000 per annum depreciation cost. The money borrowed is £100,000 at 10% cost of capital, i.e. another £10,000. Option 2 has £40,000 investment which is £4,000 depreciation plus £4,000 interest. Added to this is the £7,000 service cost. Under both options it is assumed that the net book value of the asset is zero after 10 years. **5**

(ii) Has to produce 18,000 tons of 1st quality which is 80% of production, therefore in total produces 22,500 tons. The extra 4,500 is divided equally between 2nd quality and scrap. **5**

(b) (i)

	Additional annual cost		Quality	Contribution (£ per ton)	Volume (tons)	Value (£)
	OPTION 1 (£20,000)		1st	(£400)	(18,000)	(£7.2m)
	80% of £7.2m = £5,760,000		1st	(£400)	(18,000)	(£7.2m)
	OPTION 2 (£15,000) £7.17m		1st	£400	18,000	£7.2m
			2nd	£50	1,000	£0.05m
	20% of £7.05m = £1,410,000		scrap	–£200	1,000	–£0.2m
	OPTION 3 (£30,000)		1st	(£400)	(18,000)	(£7.2m)
	OPTION 4 (£ —)		1st	(£400)	(18,000)	(£7.2m)
			2nd	(£50)	(2,250)	(£112,500)
			scrap	(£200)	(2,250)	(–£450,000)

EXPECTED VALUES

Option 1 ......£7,180,000......
Option 2 ......£7,155,000......
Option 3 ......£7,170,000......
Option 4 ......£6,862,500......

8

(ii) See completed decision tree. **4**

(iii) Option 1 as it gives the highest expected value. **1**

(iv) Option 1 not only gives the best returns but it does not have the difficulties of the other options. Option 2 has a chance of failure. It also has a service cost which may increase in price in future. Option 3 has constraints due to the water company's regulations. It also has the bad publicity issue. Falling sales and protests could result from this option. Option 4, like Option 2, has the possibility of poor quality product damaging the firm's reputation with customers. Many firms these days feel the need to get the product right first time, every time. **7**

Examiner's tip

The candidate has used all the numerical and textual information well. The calculations are set out clearly.

Mark scheme

1 (a) (i) £20,000 = £10,000 depreciation (straight line over 10 years) + £10,000 cost of capital = 2 marks

£15,000 = £4,000 depreciation (straight line over 10 years) + £4,000 cost of capital + £7,000 Service Cost = 2 marks   *5 marks*

(ii) Total output = 22,500
First quality = 18,000 (80% of 22,500)
Remainder = 4,500, half second quality, half recycled   *5 marks*

(b) (i)

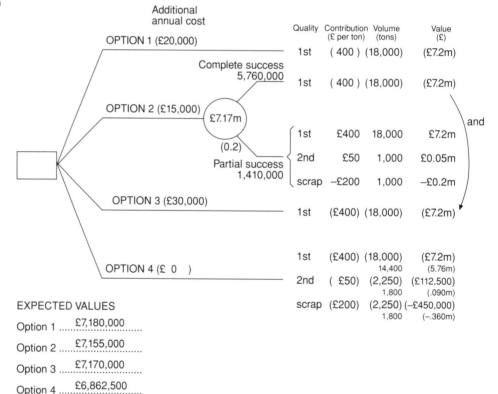

EXPECTED VALUES
Option 1 .... £7,180,000
Option 2 .... £7,155,000
Option 3 .... £7,170,000
Option 4 .... £6,862,500

8 marks

(ii) Correct answer or own figure rule applies to correct method.   *4 marks*

(iii) Option 1.   *1 mark*

(iv) Possible answers include: quality, cost, customers' attitudes, competitor actions, EU directions, legislation, pressure groups.

LEVEL 1
Relevant factors identified.   *1–3 marks*

LEVEL 2
Relevant factors explained.   *4–7 marks*

Maximum 30 marks

2 (a) Critical path analysis allows a company to work out the most efficient use of time and resources. It breaks down a project into its key activities and determines the order in which they should be done. It helps identify for a firm which activities are most important and which may hold up production if not carried out on time. **6**

(b) (i)

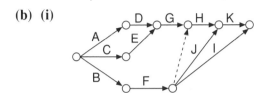

12

(ii)

	Duration	Earliest start time	Earliest finish time	Latest start time	Latest finish time	Total float	Free float
A	3	0	3	0	3	0	0
B	3	0	3	6	9	6	0
C	2	0	2	0	2	0	0
D	4	3	7	3	7	0	0
E	5	2	7	2	7	0	0
F	7	3	10	9	16	6	0
G	12	7	19	7	19	0	0
H	3	19	22	19	22	0	0
J	6	10	16	16	22	6	6
K	6	22	28	22	28	0	0
L	10	10	20	18	28	8	8

8

(iii) Critical path is A, D, G, H, K and C, E, G, H, K. **2**

Examiner's tip

This is an excellent answer. It was a very good idea to convert the table provided in the question to show the results.

(c) (i) Activities H and K are the critical activities that follow activity G. They are the only hope of saving time to make up for the two-day over-run on activity G. The firm can only reduce either activity by one day and that will cost £100 in the case of H and £150 in the case of K. **6**

(ii) The fact that any delay will invoke penalty payments is a crucial factor in making this decision. If the penalty payments are greater than the money spent on completing the project in time then the expenditure will have to be incurred, i.e. if the penalty is greater than £250 the firm will lose more if it does not complete on time. Even if the penalty payments are lower than the increased costs they may decide to pay the costs. This is because their relationship with the customer is important. Meeting the customer's needs may lead to repeat sales. **8**

(d) Making two assumptions, one that the two sub-contractors behave in the future in the same way as they behaved in the past, and two that they do not affect each other, then the probabilities are:

(i) The first sub-contractor has a probability of being late one in five times and the photographer one in ten. If we multiply these together the chances of them being both late are one in fifty. **4**

(ii) The chances of either of them being late are as follows:
The sub-contractor being late is 1/5 × 9/10 (the probability of the photographer being on time) which equals 9/50. We add this to the sub-contractor being on time 4/5 × 1/10 (the photographer being late) which is 4/50. The chances are then 9/50 + 4/50 = 13/50.   **4**

Examiner's tip

The assumptions are stated clearly as requested. This is always useful even when not asked for specifically.

Mark scheme

2 (a) LEVEL 1
Brief description of advantages.   *1–3 marks*
LEVEL 2
Explains advantages.   *4–6 marks*

(b) (i) LEVEL 1
An attempt at diagram, generally sound.   *1–7 marks*
LEVEL 2
Good diagram with correct features.   *8–12 marks*

(ii) 4 marks each.   *8 marks*

(iii) 1 mark for each critical path.   *2 marks*

(c) (i) LEVEL 1
Identifies H and K.   *2 marks*
LEVEL 2
Calculates cost of H and K.   *4 marks*
LEVEL 3
Explains costs and reasons for crashing H and K.   *6 marks*

(ii) LEVEL 1
Ideas identified.   *0–2 marks*
LEVEL 2
Ideas developed.   *3–5 marks*
LEVEL 3
Analysis and evaluation of factors.   *6–8 marks*

(d) Sub-contractor A late 1 in 5.
Sub-contractor B late 2 in 20.

(i) Both late = 1/5 × 1/10
                   = 1/50, or 2%

(ii) Either late = [1/5 × 9/10] + [4/5 × 1/10]
                     = 9/50 + 4/50
                     = 13/50, 26%   *4 marks*

LEVEL 1
Correct method.   *1–2 marks*
LEVEL 2
Correct method and calculations.   *3–4 marks*

Maximum 50 marks

3 (a) (i) Average price rises to £21
Volume falls to 4.5
Total revenue falls to £94.5m
Total direct costs fall to £58.5m
Total indirect costs stay at £25m
Net profit rises to £11m   **7**

(ii) Total revenue stays at £92m
Direct materials fall to £19m
Direct labour rises to £14m
Direct production rises to £18m
Total direct costs fall to £51m
Depreciation rises to £9m
Total indirect costs rise to £28m
Net profit rises to £13m   **7**

Examiner's tip

The candidate picks up all the relevant information in the question and sets it out clearly.

(b) Labour production and depreciation costs rise by £4m but direct materials cost £8m less which gives a net increase in profits of £4m. The firm has gained the advantage of lower materials costs by absorbing the profit the original component manufacturer was making. Another two advantages of this strategy are that supplies of these components can now be guaranteed, whereas the original component manufacturer could have let Multiproducts down at some point in the future. Ownership of the component company may also deny a competitor access to these components.   **7**

(c) This would be a major strategic decision. The firm would lose some control over the assembly of the product. It would have to be very confident about the quality and reliability of the sub-contractor. The sub-contractor would have to offer significant benefits, e.g. reduced prices (due to economies of scale) to justify such a decision. **4**

Mark scheme

3 (a)

	Product line 1	*Product line 2*
Average price	21.0	23.0
Volume	4.5	4.0
Total revenue	94.5	92.0
Direct materials	27.0	19.0
Direct labour	18.0	14.0
Direct production	13.5	18.0
Total direct cost	58.5	51.0
Indirect labour	10.0	12.0
Depreciation	10.0	9.0
Marketing	3.0	4.0
R & D	1.0	2.0
Administration	1.0	1.0
Total indirect costs	25.0	28.0
Net profit	11.0	13.0

(i) and (ii) 1 mark for each correct change or 7 marks for correct net profit.

(b) Possible answers include: cost savings, not paying suppliers' profit margin. Advantages include guaranteed supply and guaranteed quality.

LEVEL 1
Correct ideas identified.   *1–3 marks*

LEVEL 2
Ideas and advantages explained.   *4–7 marks*

(c) Answers include:
Contractors' prices – would they rise or fall? Lack of control. Other costs.

LEVEL 1
Two points identified.   *1–2 marks*

LEVEL 2
Two points explained.   *3–4 marks*

                                                                            Maximum 25 marks

4 (a) (i) In the short term the firm's losses on duvet covers will increase because it will not be possible to reduce the fixed overhead costs. This will therefore put the whole firm into a loss-making position because the firm will have lost £120,000 worth of revenue from not selling duvet covers and it will have only saved £102,000 worth of costs on making duvet covers. Taking this £18,000 from the current profit of £13,400 gives a loss of £4,600.   **6**

Examiner's tip

The candidate picked up the key clue in the question that fixed costs were unaltered.

(ii) In the long term it may be possible to save on the fixed overheads, putting the company back into a profit-making position. However, this may be difficult if the duvet covers are made on the same site as the pillow-cases and fitted sheets. Unless a new product is found, they will be stuck with unused capacity. This could have a significant impact on the long-term viability of the company. They may have problems in terms of labour morale as they will have to shed labour. They may have problems with customers switching to other manufacturers who produce a complete range of bedding.   **4**

(b) One option is to try to increase the revenue gained from duvet covers. Depending on the price elasticity of demand, this may be either by lowering or raising the price of the duvet covers. As the products are of high quality it may be that sufficient customers would continue to buy the product even if the price was raised. If they raise the price 5% and demand fell only 1% then revenue would increase. Alternatively, if demand was price-elastic, it might be as well to go slightly down-market, diversifying into other market segments.

If they lowered the price 10% and demand increased by 50% then revenue would rise. Another option for the company is to try to reduce its costs. Direct materials costs could be reduced by buying cheaper materials and labour costs could be reduced by introducing more automation.   **6**

Examiner's tip

The candidate has helped the Examiner by distinguishing between alternatives in one option and looking at a second option as requested.

(c) It is crucial to the decision-making process that firms should have shared and clear aims. Once decision makers know what they are aiming to achieve they should seek to gather all the information needed to help make the decision. Once they have the information, they should look in detail at alternative solutions. They then must choose one of the alternatives. The solution should be planned carefully and then implemented. Both during and after the implementation phase it must be evaluated and then the whole cycle starts again.   **6**

Mark scheme

4 **(a)** **(i)** Identified up to three short-term implications.   *1–3 marks*
  Gave brief explanation in the context of Watcher Limited.   *1–3 marks*

  Possible answers: Loss of sales income £170,000 *(1 mark)*. Saving in costs £102,000 *(1 mark)*. Fall in profits £18,000 *(1 mark)*. Current profit £13,400 – £18,000 = (£4,600) loss *(1 mark)*. Explanation *(2 marks)*.
  Total income without duvets:
  £170,000 *(1 mark)*.
  Direct materials £50,000.
  Direct labour £60,000.
  Variable overheads £17,500.
  Total variable costs £127,500 *(1 mark)*.
  Contribution £42,500 *(1 mark)*.
  Fixed costs £47,100.
  Loss (£4,600) *(1 mark)*
  Explanation of the above *(2 marks)*.

  Other possible answers: Effects on sales of other products/retailers may switch to competitors. Effects on staff/redundancy/morale/industrial action. Effects on stocks/waste/discounts from suppliers. Effects on production capacity/ depreciation/ sales of assets. Financial implications/loss of income/fixed costs spread over smaller output/average costs rise/cash flow/attitude of the bank.

  (ii) Identified up to two implications in long term.

  Possible answers: Sales may continue to fall/capacity problems grow/contribution loss/profits disappear/firm goes bust. Some blurring between short and long term. Marks cannot be gained for repeating information.
                                         1–2 marks for each implication up to a maximum of 4

 (b) Increase or decrease price/redesign product/reduce labour content/reduce materials/ different market segments/sell entire range based on market research/diversify/ reduce costs/better labour utilisation/automation.

                                                        Identified up to two options 1–2 marks
                                                          Simple development of each 1–2 marks
                                                          Further development of each 1–2 marks

 (c) Be clear about objectives/gather all relevant data/both internally and externally/clearly define problem/distinguish causes from symptoms/develop range of options/solutions/ evaluate alternatives/choose most appropriate option/implement, monitor and control/ then start loop again.

                                                  1 mark for each point up to a maximum of 6
                                                  Reward for diagram of decision-making loop
                                                                    Maximum 22 marks

Acknowledgements

The author and publishers gratefully acknowledge the following for permission to use questions, text and figures in this book:

Questions

Questions 1, 2, 3, 4, 5, 6, 7, 8 (Unit 1); 3, 4, 5 (Unit 2); 3, 4 (Unit 3); 4, 5, 6 (Unit 4); 1, 2, 3, 4, 6 (Unit 5) 1, 2, 3, 4, 6, 7 (Unit 6); and 3, 4 (Unit 7): Reproduced by kind permission of the Associated Examining Board. Any answers or hints on answers are the sole responsibility of the author and have not been provided or approved by the Board. Questions 1 (Unit 3); 5 (Unit 5); 5 (Unit 6); and 1, 2 (Unit 7): Reproduced by permission of the University of Cambridge Local Examinations Syndicate. The University of Cambridge Local Examinations Syndicate bears no responsibility for the example answers to questions taken from its past question papers which are contained in this publication. Questions 1, 2 (Unit 2) and 2 (Unit 3): Reproduced by kind permission of the Northern Examinations and Assessment Board. The author accepts responsibility for answers provided, which may not necessarily constitute the only possible solutions. Questions 1, 2, 3 (Unit 4): © Northern Ireland Council for the Curriculum, Examinations and Assessment 1995. Questions 5 (Unit 3) and 8 (Unit 6): Reproduced by kind permission of the Oxford and Cambridge Schools Examination Board. Question 7 (Unit 5): Reproduced by kind permission of the Scottish Examination Board. Answers are the sole responsibility of the author and have not been provided by the Board.

Text and figures

p8 article adapted from 'New Power to Innovators' by Marion Devine, The Sunday Times, 14 August 1988, © Marion Devine; p9 'The Universe of Franchising' adapted from an article by Derek Ayling, Management Today, April 1988 (diagram reproduced by permission of Power Research Associates); p15 'After 31 years the Mini keeps on growing' by Kevin Eason, adapted and reprinted with permission from The Sunday Times, 22 December 1990, © Times Newspapers Limited, 1990; p16 'Mineral waters in the UK', The Quarterly Review of Marketing, Summer 1989, by permission of the Chartered Institute of Marketing (table based on Perrier UK estimates); p20 table from Social Trends 1995. Crown copyright 1995. Reproduced by the permission of the Controller of HMSO and the Central Statistical Office; pp20–1 extracts adapted from *Quality Circles in Action* by M Robson, published by Gower, reprinted by permission of Gower Publishing Ltd; p21 graph adapted from Personnel Today, January 1993; p22 'Euro Disney loses visitors – and £30m' by Lisa Buckingham, 20 November 1992, © The Guardian 1992; p23 'Disney takes white-knuckle ride as the cash fails to flow' by Martin Waller, The Times, © Times Newspapers Limited, 09 July 1993; p24 'Castles in cold air: Euro Disney needs several transformation scenes', October 1993, © The Guardian; p24 'Euro Disney future in doubt' by Helen Davidson, The Sunday Times, © Times Newspapers Limited, 15 August 1993; p25 'One out of ten jobs to go at Euro Disneyland' by Martin Waller, The Times, © Times Newspapers Limited, 19 October 1993; p29 Cadbury Schweppes' 1989 results reprinted by permission of Cadbury Schweppes plc; p36 'Prime movers' adapted from *Venture* Vol 2, No 6, Autumn 1990, reproduced by permission of Aston Science Park; p40 from 'Petrol Prices: The Facts', a leaflet distributed by BP Oil UK Ltd in 1992, reprinted with permission; p43 'Producing a Recovery' adapted from an article in the Lloyds Bank Economic Bulletin, No 173, May 1993, reprinted by permission of Lloyds Bank (graph based on CSO data. Crown copyright. Reproduced by the permission of the Controller of HMSO and the Central Statistical Office.); p44 'Paper cups may be more damaging to the environment than their polystyrene rivals' by Nick Nuttall, The Times, © Times Newspapers Limited, 14 February 1991; p45 'Did you know?' Fact sheet no 2 produced by McDonald's Public Relations Department, 01/90, reprinted by permission of McDonald's Restaurants Ltd.